THE GREAT SEAL OF THE STATE OF CALIFORNIA

EUREKA

CALIFORNIA VISTAS

PEOPLE AND PLACES

James A. Banks, Ph.D.

Kevin P. Colleary, Ed.D.

Stephen F. Cunha, Ph.D.

Jana Echevarria, Ph.D.

Walter C. Parker, Ph.D.

James J. Rawls, Ph.D.

Rosalía Salinas

Emily M. Schell, Ed.D.

PROGRAM AUTHORS

James A. Banks, Ph.D.
Russell F. Stark University
  Professor and Director, Center
  for Multicultural Education
University of Washington
Seattle, Washington

Kevin P. Colleary, Ed.D.
Curriculum and Teaching
  Department
Graduate School of Education
Fordham University
New York, New York

Stephen F. Cunha, Ph.D.
Professor of Geography
Humboldt State University
Arcata, California

Jana Echevarria, Ph.D.
Professor, College of Education
California State University
Long Beach, California

Walter C. Parker, Ph.D.
Professor of Education and
  Chair of Social Studies Education
University of Washington
Seattle, Washington

James J. Rawls, Ph.D.
Department of History
Diablo Valley College
Pleasant Hill, California

Rosalía Salinas
Senior Director
Learning Resources and Educational
  Technology Division (retired)
San Diego County Office
  of Education
San Diego, California

Emily M. Schell, Ed.D.
Social Studies Education Director,
City Heights Educational
  Collaborative
Visiting Professor, Teacher Education
San Diego State University
San Diego, California

 **California Geographic
Alliance**
Humboldt State University
Arcata, California

HISTORIANS/SCHOLARS

Amrik Singh Dua, Ph.D.
Professor and Department Chair
Dept. of Business Administration
Mount San Antonio College
Walnut, California

Paula S. Fass, Ph.D.
Margaret Byrne Professor of History
University of California
Berkeley, California

Don R. Leet, Ph.D.
Chair, Economics Department
Director of the Center for
  Economic Education
California State University
Fresno, California

Mary Ting Yi Lui, Ph.D.
Assistant Professor of History
  and American Studies
Yale University
New Haven, Connecticut

James M. McPherson, Ph.D.
George Henry Davis '86 Professor of
  American History, Emeritus
Princeton University
Princeton, New Jersey

Karen Nakai, Ed.D.
Professor, College of Education
California State University
Long Beach, California

Curtis C. Roseman, Ph.D.
Professor Emeritus of Geography
University of Southern California
Los Angeles, California

Clifford E. Trafzer, Ph.D.
Professor of American Indian History
University of California
Riverside, California

CONSULTANTS

Primary Sources Research
Library of Congress
Publishing Office
Washington, D.C.

Reading and Writing
Adria F. Klein, Ph.D.
Professor Emeritus
California State University
San Bernardino, California

English Learners
Elizabeth Jimenez
Pomona, California

GRADE LEVEL CONSULTANTS AND REVIEWERS

Monica Kibbe
Second Grade Teacher
Brisbane Elementary School
Brisbane, California

Sarab Lopes
Second Grade Teacher
Anza Elementary School
El Cajon, California

Pamela McGregor
Project Coordinator, Teaching
  American History
San Diego County Office
  of Education
San Diego, California

Bev Farrell-Smith
Second Grade Teacher
Mitchell Elementary School
Santa Clarita, California

Cynthia Vaughn
Elementary School Teacher
Rooftop Alternative School
San Francisco, California

Maria de los Angeles Villa
Second Grade Teacher
Roosevelt Elementary School
Pomona, California

CALIFORNIA EDITORIAL ADVISORY BOARD

Ginger Borror
Sixth Grade Teacher
Easterby Elementary School
Fresno, California

Tim Broader
Elementary Teacher, Grades 3–6
Susan B. Anthony Elementary School
Fresno, California

Kathleen Brown
Sixth Grade Teacher
Mitchell Community
  Elementary School
Santa Clarita, California

Stephanie Buttell-Maxin
Third Grade Teacher
Kimball Elementary School
National City, California

Dr. Tina Cantrell
Former Curriculum Director
Assistant/Associate Superintendent
Moorpark Unified School District
Moorpark, California

Marlene Dane
Third Grade Teacher
Bonita Canyon School
Irvine, California

Bev Farrell-Smith
Second Grade Teacher
Mitchell Community
  Elementary School
Santa Clarita, California

Victoria Ford
Project Administrator
Monte Vista Elementary School
Montclair, California

Debra Gallagher
First Grade GATE
74th Street Elementary School
Los Angeles, California

Michael Haggood
Principal
Los Angeles Unified
  School District
Los Angeles, California

Bill Laraway
Fifth Grade Teacher
Silver Oak Elementary School
San José, California

Sheri Nagel
Superintendent of Schools
Central School District
Rancho Cucamonga, California

Dr. Janet Scott
Principal
Peres Elementary
Richmond, California

Maria de los Angeles Villa
Second Grade Teacher
Roosevelt Elementary School
Pomona, California

Doua Vu
Resource Specialist
Office of State and Federal
  Programs/Title III
Fresno Unified School District
Fresno, California

Claudia West
Third Grade Teacher
Westlake Hills Elementary
Westlake Village, California

 RFB&D
learning through listening

Students with print disabilities
may be eligible to obtain
an accessible, audio version
of the pupil edition of
this textbook. Please call
Recording for the Blind &
Dyslexic at 1-800-221-4792
for complete information.

A

The McGraw·Hill Companies

**Macmillan
McGraw-Hill**

Published by Macmillan/McGraw-Hill, of McGraw-Hill Education, a division of the McGraw-Hill Companies, Inc., Two Penn Plaza, New York, New York 10121.

Printed in the United States of America

ISBN 0-02-150509-8

1 2 3 4 5 6 7 8 XXX 08 07 06 05

★ CONTENTS ★

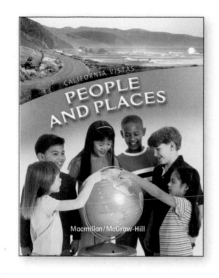

UNIT 4

Our Needs and Wants 217

Reference Section

Skills and Features

Reading Social Studies

Using Primary Sources

Chart and Graph Skills

Critical Thinking Skills

Map and Globe Skills

Study and Research Skills

Biography

Citizenship

Being a Good Citizen

Democracy in Action

Literature

Skills and Features

Charts, Graphs, and Diagrams

Maps

Primary Source Quotes

Start with Your
CALIFORNIA STANDARDS

★☆★

California standards tell you the most important things you need to learn while studying social studies. There is a complete list of these standards at the end of this book.

California standards are shown on many different pages. Look at the first page from Unit 2 below. Read the words in the light blue box to find the California standard.

This is where you can find the California standard.

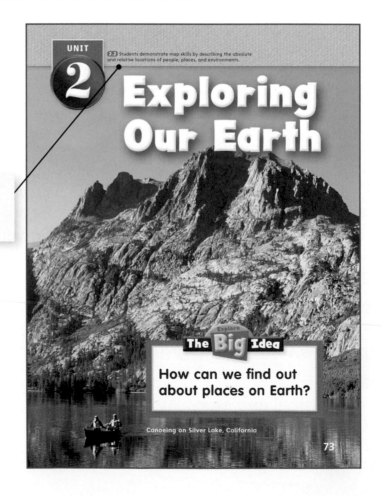

UNIT

2

2.2 Students demonstrate map skills by describing the absolute and relative locations of people, places, and environments.

Exploring Our Earth

The **Big** Idea

How can we find out about places on Earth?

Canoeing on Silver Lake, California

73

About

The Big Idea

You will also find Big Idea questions in your book. They are important social studies questions.

There are five units in your book. Each unit has its own Big Idea question. Here is the same first page from Unit 2. Read the words in the light blue box to find the Big Idea question on the page.

This is the Big Idea question.

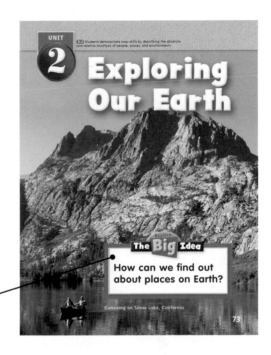

On the last page of each unit is a Big Idea Activity. It is a fun way to show all that you have learned about the Big Idea.

This is the Big Idea Activity.

Your book has many different pages. Here are some of the kinds of pages you will find.

Each unit begins with pages that tell more about the Big Idea question. They are called the Big Idea pages. You can learn more about the Big Idea question by reading these pages. See the Big Idea pages for Unit 2 below.

UNIT

2

The Explore **Big Idea**

How can we find out about places on Earth?

Vocabulary

geography
globe

The word **geography** comes from two word parts. The part "geo" means *Earth*. The part "graphy" means *to tell about* or *write*. Geography tells about the things that make up our Earth.

"A globe is a model of Earth. I use a globe to learn about the land and water that make up Earth."

"A map tells me how to find places."

"I can explore Earth. I can look at things in nature."

In this unit you will discover geography. You will find out about many places on Earth. You will learn how to use different kinds of maps.

74

75

UNIT **2** **Literature**

The Treasure Hunt

by Becky Manfredini and Jenny Reznick
illustrated by Obadinah Heavner

It's time for a treasure hunt.
Here's what to do.
Follow the trail.
It's up to you!

76

▲ **Each unit starts with a story, poem, or song.**

UNIT **2** **Vocabulary**
About Geography

Read the words in the boxes. Then look at the pictures.

An **urban** area is a city. (page 90)

A **suburban** area is an area near a city. (page 91)

80

▲ **You learn new vocabulary words in every unit.**

▼ **Each unit has many lessons. You will learn new things in each lesson.**

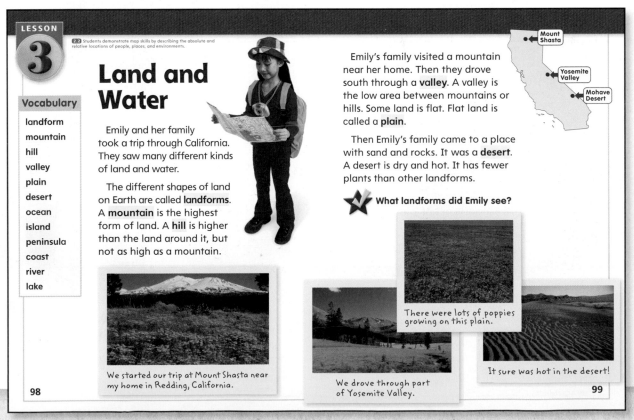

LESSON **3**

2.2 Students demonstrate map skills by describing the absolute and relative locations of people, places, and environments.

Land and Water

Vocabulary

landform
mountain
hill
valley
plain
desert
ocean
island
peninsula
coast
river
lake

Emily and her family took a trip through California. They saw many different kinds of land and water.

The different shapes of land on Earth are called **landforms**. A **mountain** is the highest form of land. A **hill** is higher than the land around it, but not as high as a mountain.

Emily's family visited a mountain near her home. Then they drove south through a **valley**. A valley is the low area between mountains or hills. Some land is flat. Flat land is called a **plain**.

Then Emily's family came to a place with sand and rocks. It was a **desert**. A desert is dry and hot. It has fewer plants than other landforms.

★ **What landforms did Emily see?**

Mount Shasta
Yosemite Valley
Mohave Desert

We started our trip at Mount Shasta near my home in Redding, California.

We drove through part of Yosemite Valley.

There were lots of poppies growing on this plain.

It sure was hot in the desert!

98

99

Skills lessons help you learn about maps, charts, graphs, and reading social studies.

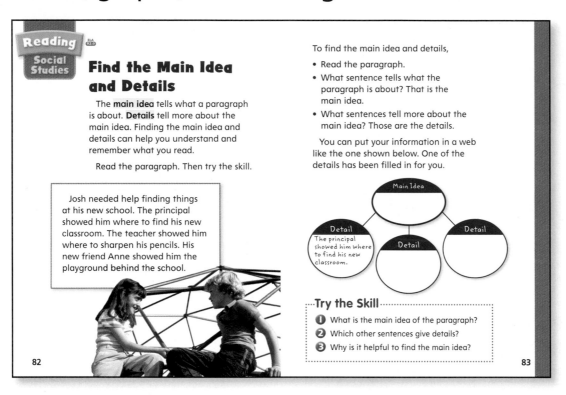

Social Studies

Find the Main Idea and Details

The **main idea** tells what a paragraph is about. **Details** tell more about the main idea. Finding the main idea and details can help you understand and remember what you read.

Read the paragraph. Then try the skill.

Josh needed help finding things at his new school. The principal showed him where to find his new classroom. The teacher showed him where to sharpen his pencils. His new friend Anne showed him the playground behind the school.

To find the main idea and details,

• Read the paragraph.
• What sentence tells what the paragraph is about? That is the main idea.
• What sentences tell more about the main idea? Those are the details.

You can put your information in a web like the one shown below. One of the details has been filled in for you.

Main Idea

Detail
The principal showed him where to find his new classroom.

Detail

Detail

Try the Skill

❶ What is the main idea of the paragraph?
❷ Which other sentences give details?
❸ Why is it helpful to find the main idea?

82   83

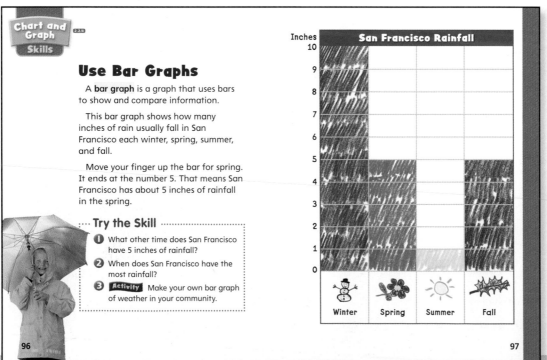

Skills

Use Bar Graphs

A **bar graph** is a graph that uses bars to show and compare information.

This bar graph shows how many inches of rain usually fall in San Francisco each winter, spring, summer, and fall.

Move your finger up the bar for spring. It ends at the number 5. That means San Francisco has about 5 inches of rainfall in the spring.

Try the Skill

❶ What other time does San Francisco have 5 inches of rainfall?
❷ When does San Francisco have the most rainfall?
❸ **Activity** Make your own bar graph of weather in your community.

San Francisco Rainfall

Inches: 10, 9, 8, 7, 6, 5, 4, 3, 2, 1, 0

Winter Spring Summer Fall

96   97

There are also special lessons. Some of these lessons tell about being honest or getting along. Others tell about important people.

Geography Handbook

A Letter from Stephen Cunha

Dear Students :

Hi. I am Stephen Cunha. I am one of the authors of this social studies book. I am also a geographer. Geographers are people who study geography. Geography is the study of Earth's surface. It is also about the plants, animals, and people who live on Earth.

Geography is an important part of social studies. The land, plants, animals, and people have changed our country. Geography is a part of our country's past.

You will read about geography in this handbook. You will learn about the five themes of geography, how to read maps, and more. You will see how geography is a part of your life!

Enjoy your travels!

Stephen Cunha
The California Geographic
Alliance

The Five Themes of Geography

Each part of our world is connected to many other parts. Some geographers divide geography into five themes, or parts. The five themes help us to see all of the parts of geography.

Location

A location is an exact spot on Earth. This fountain in Horton Park, San Diego, is a location.

Place

A place can be any area. Some places are mountains and rivers. Other places are cities and roads.

Region

A region is a large area that is the same in some way. Many regions share the same weather and landforms. A region is bigger than a place or area.

Movement

Movement means to change from one place or position to another. People travel from one area to another. Truck drivers carry things from one area to another.

People Change the Land

Geographers look to see how people change the land. For example, when many people move to an area, they build roads, cities, factories, buildings, and houses.

Dictionary of Geographic Words

DESERT—Hot, dry area that has few plants

HILL—Land that is higher than the land around it, but not as high as a mountain

PENINSULA—Land that has water on all sides but one

LAKE—Body of water with land all around it

OCEAN—Largest body of water

ISLAND—Land that has water all around it

MOUNTAIN—Highest kind of land

VALLEY—Low land between hills or mountains

RIVER—A single stream of water that flows into a larger body of water

PLAIN—Flat land

Reviewing Geography Skills
Use Directions

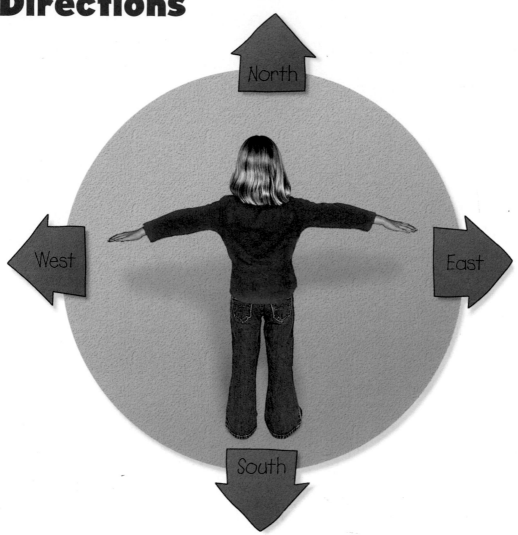

A direction is any way you can face or point. There are four main directions. They are north, south, east, and west. Directions help us answer the question, "Where is it?" Directions also help us to find where something is on a map.

 What direction does the girl's right hand point toward?

Use Addresses

An address is a location. It tells where a house or building is located. An address has a number and a street name. The address of this house is 2 Elm Street.

 What is the address of your house?

Use Photographs and Maps

Look at the photograph on this page. It is a picture from the air. It shows a neighborhood.

A map is a drawing of a place. The drawing on the next page is a map of the neighborhood in this photograph.

This map shows the same houses, garages, driveways, and streets as in the photograph. You could use this map to find a place in the neighborhood.

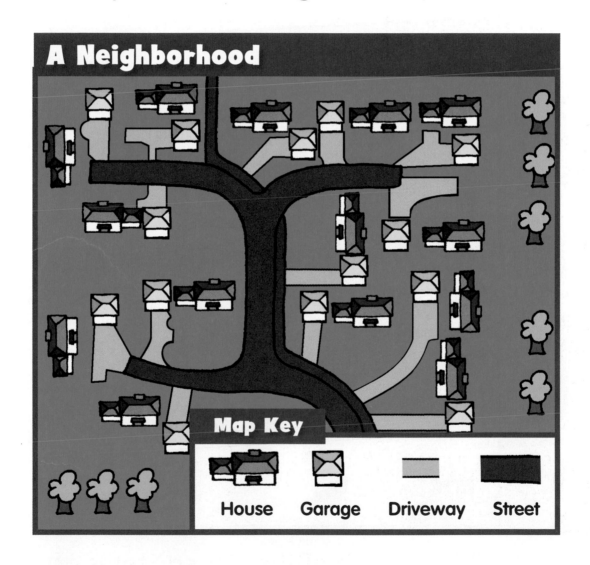

A Neighborhood

Map Key

House	Garage	Driveway	Street

 How are the map and the photograph alike? How are they different?

Read Maps

The United States of America

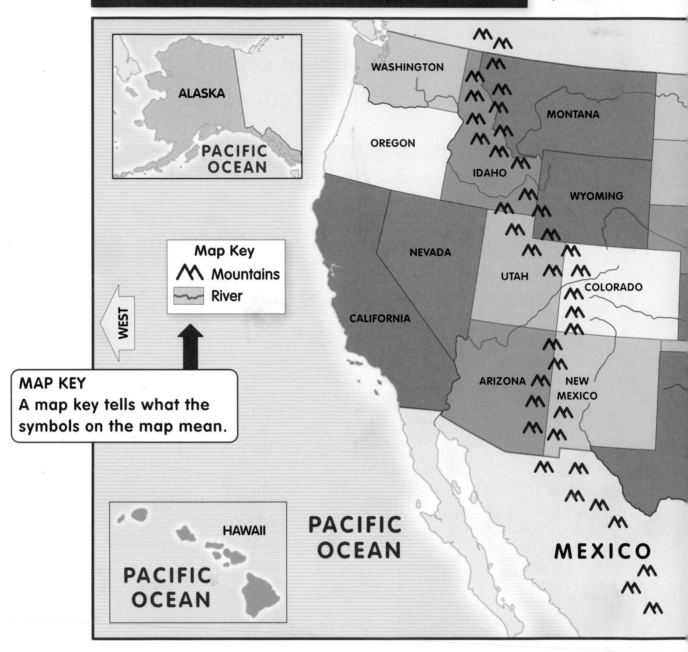

MAP KEY
A map key tells what the symbols on the map mean.

Map Key
- Mountains
- River

This is a map of the United States of America. The United States of America is our **country**. A country is a land and the people who live there. Our country is made up of 50 **states**. A state is one part of a country.

TITLE
The title is the name of the map.
It tells you what the map shows.

NORTH

CANADA

NEW HAMPSHIRE

VERMONT

MAINE

NORTH DAKOTA

MINNESOTA

MICHIGAN

NEW YORK

MASSACHUSETTS

RHODE ISLAND

CONNECTICUT

SOUTH DAKOTA

WISCONSIN

NEW JERSEY

DELAWARE

MARYLAND

NEBRASKA

IOWA

PENNSYLVANIA

OHIO

ILLINOIS

INDIANA

KANSAS

MISSOURI

KENTUCKY

WEST VIRGINIA

VIRGINIA

EAST

ARKANSAS

TENNESSEE

NORTH CAROLINA

OKLAHOMA

SOUTH CAROLINA

MISSISSIPPI

ALABAMA

GEORGIA

ATLANTIC OCEAN

LOUISIANA

TEXAS

FLORIDA

DIRECTIONS
Maps give you directions.
They tell you which way
is north, south, east
and west on the map.

SOUTH

Most maps have a title, map key, and
directions. These three things help us
read and use maps.

**What direction would you go to get from
the state of Washington to California?**

Picture Earth

This photograph was taken from outer space. It is a picture of Earth. Earth looks like a big ball. The blue areas are oceans. The brown and green areas are land. The white swirls are clouds.

The bright area is the country where you live. It is the United States of America.

Earth

A **globe** is a special map that is shaped like a ball. It is a small model of Earth. A model is a copy of something. A globe shows what the land and water look like on Earth.

You can see a line around the widest part of the globe. This is the equator. The equator is an imaginary line. It separates north from south on Earth.

Equator

Globe

 Is the United States north or south of the equator?

Use History Maps

A history map tells about a place in the past. Read the map title to learn what the map shows.

This map tells a story about the **Pilgrims**. The Pilgrims were people from the country of England. They sailed on a ship to America a long time ago. Their ship was called the *Mayflower*. This map shows the path that the Pilgrims took when they sailed on the *Mayflower* from England to America.

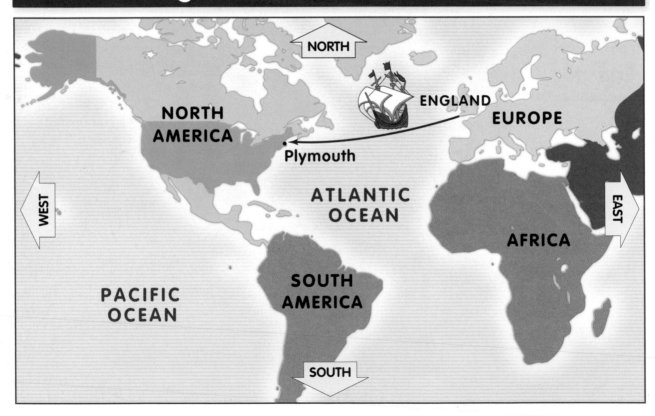

The Pilgrims Sail to America, 1620

NORTH

NORTH AMERICA

ENGLAND

EUROPE

WEST

Plymouth

ATLANTIC OCEAN

EAST

AFRICA

PACIFIC OCEAN

SOUTH AMERICA

SOUTH

What direction did the Pilgrims travel when they came from England to America?

UNIT

1

2.1 Students differentiate between things that happened long ago and things that happened yesterday.

Families Long Ago

The Explore Big Idea

How did families long ago make a difference in our world today?

American family from the early 1900s

Explore
The Big Idea

How did families long ago make a difference in our world today?

History is the story of the past. Every family has its own history. Read about what these families did long ago.

"Our family was the first to change this land into a farm."

"Our family came to America to make a better life."

"Our family was the first to build a home in this California neighborhood."

"Our families marched to change laws that were not fair."

Families long ago made a difference in our world today. In this unit you will learn more about family history.

Literature

Children of Long Ago

by Lessie Jones Little
illustrated by Deborah White

The children who lived a long time ago
In little country towns
Ate picnics under spreading trees,
Played hopscotch on the cool dirt yards,
Picked juicy grapes from broad
   grapevines,
Pulled beets and potatoes
   from the ground,
Those children of long ago.

The children who lived a long time ago
In little country towns
Decked themselves in their Sunday best,
Went to church and visited friends,
Sang happy songs with their mamas
    and papas,
Traveled through books for sights
    and sounds,
Those children of long ago.

Talk About It!

Talk about something you do today that children did long ago.

5

Vocabulary
About History

Read the words in the boxes. Then find the pictures in the big photographs.

Native Americans were the first people to live in America. (page 38)

Pilgrims were a group of people from England who traveled to America. (page 42)

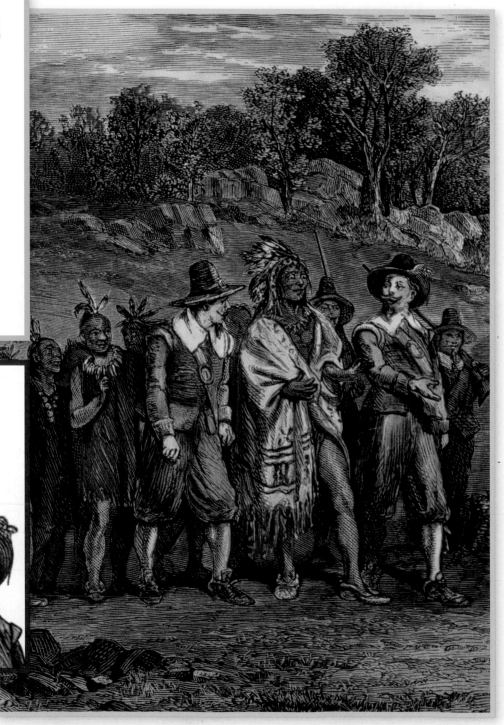

Immigrants are people who leave one country to live in another. (page 54)

Write About It! What do you see in these pictures?

Compare and Contrast

Things can be alike and different. We **compare** things to find how they are alike. We **contrast** things to find how they are different.

To compare and contrast,

- Pick two ideas or people from a paragraph or picture.
- Compare them by finding things about them that are alike.
- Contrast them by finding things about them that are different.

You can put your information in a Venn diagram like the one shown below.

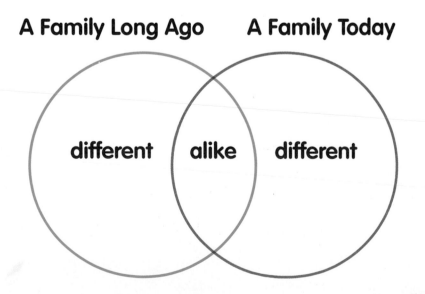

A Family Long Ago   A Family Today

different   alike   different

Look at the pictures. Then try the skill.

A family long ago

A family today

·· Try the Skill ································

1 How are these two families alike?

2 How are these two families different?

3 Why is it helpful to compare and contrast?

2.1.2 Compare and contrast their daily lives with those of their parents, grandparents, and/or guardians.

Family Traditions

Vocabulary

traditions

Have you ever wondered what the members of your family did when they were growing up? Many families have **traditions**. A tradition is a special way of doing something that is passed down over time.

Yoshi's grandfather is from Japan. In Japan he learned how to eat with chopsticks. Now he can show Yoshi.

Elsa wears colorful striped socks. She also wears shoes called clogs. The socks and clogs were gifts from her grandmother. Elsa's grandmother is from the Netherlands. Her grandmother also wore socks and clogs when she was a young girl.

 What traditions does your family have?

Crafts and Food

Lela's family has been living in California for a long, long time. Lela's mother teaches her how to make a basket with feathers, shell beads, and glass beads.

Making baskets is a family tradition. Lela's mother is making sure that this tradition is not forgotten.

Hatim eats a delicious pita sandwich stuffed with vegetables. Hatim's uncle learned to make pita sandwiches when he was a boy in Libya. Now he shows Hatim how to make them.

Many of the foods we like to eat come from all over the world. Families pass down these traditions so their children can enjoy these foods too.

 How does a tradition get passed down?

Hupa baskets

Stories and Music

Mrs. Etana's family comes from West Africa. She likes to share stories about the village her family came from.

Mrs. Etana says that village stories were first passed down by *griots*. A griot is a person who learns stories by memory and then tells them to others.

Today griots still tell stories and sing songs about life in West Africa.

Luke enjoys playing the guitar. Luke's father taught him how to play a kind of Mexican music called *mariachi*. Luke's grandfather was in a mariachi band in Mexico.

Luke and his father like to play for their friends and family. They know they are keeping an important tradition alive.

Why is a griot's job important?

Lesson Review

1. What are traditions?

Big Idea 2. Why is knowing about your family history important?

3. **Compare and Contrast** How are the traditions of making baskets and making pita sandwiches alike? How are they different?

Understanding Photographs

A photograph is a picture that is taken with a camera. It is a copy of something. Photographs can show us what something really looked like long ago. This is a photograph of a wedding that took place long ago.

Look Closely

- The photograph on the next page is in black and white.

- The hair styles and clothing are different than what we wear today.

- A wedding is happy, but the people are not smiling.

Long ago, cameras did not take color photographs. People had to sit or stand still waiting for the camera to work. It was hard to keep a smile for such a long time!

Primary Source Review

1 What is a photograph?

2 How can you tell that the photograph is old?

3 What do you think a photograph of a wedding today would look like?

Use a Compass Rose

Look at the map on the next page. There is a special symbol on this map called a **compass rose**. A compass rose has arrows that point to the letters **N**, **S**, **E**, and **W**. These arrows show the directions north, south, east, and west.

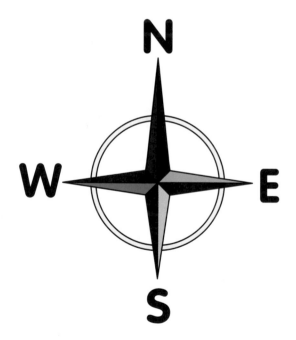

Find Mount Shasta on the map. Now find Redding. Look at the compass rose. It shows you that Redding is south of Mount Shasta.

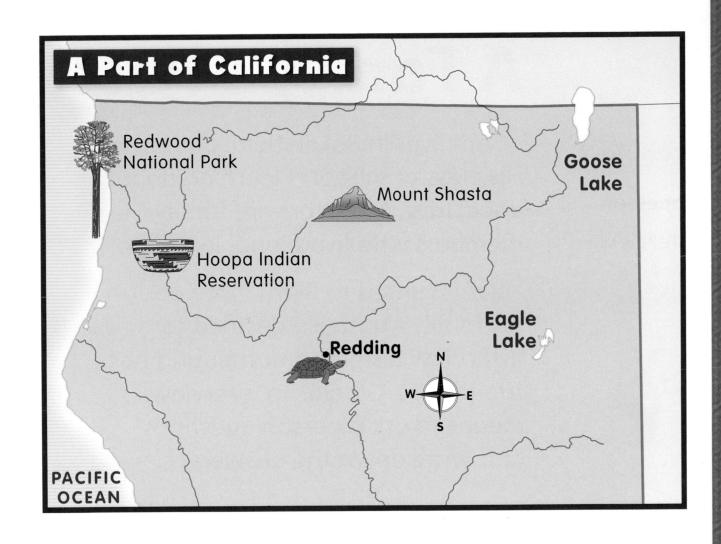

A Part of California

Redwood National Park

Mount Shasta

Goose Lake

Hoopa Indian Reservation

Eagle Lake

• Redding

N
W — E
S

PACIFIC OCEAN

Try the Skill

1. What lake is south of Goose Lake?

2. Is Eagle Lake east or west of the Hoopa Indian Reservation?

3. Is Redwood National Park on the east or west side of the map?

A Family's Past

Vocabulary

ancestor

interview

Sam lives in Bakersfield, California. His class at school is learning about **ancestors**. Ancestors are family members who lived long, long ago.

Sam wanted to learn more about his family's past. He decided to **interview** his grandmother and her friend, Mrs. Garcia. To interview means to ask a person questions and write down the answers.

Here is what was said in the interview.

Sam: Grandma, where did you live when you were a girl?

Grandma: I grew up on a farm in Virginia in the 1930s.

Sam: Is this a picture of your farm?

Grandma: Yes, it is. I worked hard on the farm. I helped my mother cook and take care of the house.

Sam: Did you do anything else?

Grandma: Sometimes I helped my brother and father plant vegetables and pick peaches from the trees.

 What is an interview?

Virginia farm in the 1930s

From Virginia to California

Sam: When did you leave the farm?

Grandma: We left when your grandpa and I got married. We wanted to start a new life together. We heard there were better jobs and good weather in California.

Sam: How did you get to California?

Grandma: We rode on a train called a streamliner. We rode through the Rocky Mountains. I could see the land all around us from the observation car.

Sam: What is an observation car?

Grandma: It is a special railway car with big glass sides that you can see out of.

Sam: That sounds like a lot of fun.

Grandma: Oh, it was! I could not believe my eyes when I saw snow on the ground in the spring!

 How did Sam's grandparents get to California?

From Mexico to California

Sam: Mrs. Garcia, did you ride a train from Virginia too?

Mrs. Garcia: I rode on a train, but not from Virginia. My family also lived on a farm. But our farm was in Oaxaca, Mexico.

Sam: Why did you leave Mexico?

Mrs. Garcia: I was ten years old. My father had trouble finding work in Mexico. Then he joined the Bracero program. The Bracero program paid men from Mexico to work on California farms. My family and I rode a train from Mexico all the way to California.

Sam: Were you afraid to leave home?

Mrs. Garcia: I sure was! I did not want to leave my home. But my father told me that we could have a better life in California. My mother helped me learn some English.

Sam: Did you like California?

Mrs. Garcia: Oh, yes! Sometimes I miss my life in Mexico. But life in California is good!

 Why did Mrs. Garcia's father join the Bracero program?

Lesson Review

1. What is an ancestor?

Big Idea

2. How did Sam's grandma's past make a difference in where Sam lives today?

3. **Compare and Contrast** How are the lives of Sam's grandma and Mrs. Garcia alike? Different?

Josefina Fierro de Bright

Josefina Fierro de Bright was born in Mexico. Her family moved to California to work on farms when she was a young girl. Josefina saw that Mexican Americans were not treated the same as other people.

When she grew up she became a leader in El Congreso. El Congreso was a group of people who worked for the rights of Mexican Americans.

Using Primary Sources

❝Mexican Americans have a long history of struggling for civil rights and freedom. We will never stop until we achieve those goals.❞

— Josefina Fierro de Bright

Mexican American children were not allowed to swim in public pools. They were not treated fairly in school. Josefina worked hard to change this.

She also helped Spanish speaking workers. Today Mexican Americans have a better life because of Josefina's fight for justice. Justice means to make things fair.

 How were Mexican American children treated unfairly?

 For more about Josefina Fierro de Bright, visit:

Use Time Lines

A **time line** is a line that shows the
order in which things have happened.

Tim's family

1920   1930   1940   1950   1960

1925

My great great
grandparents
moved here
from Scotland.

1958

My grandmother
is holding my mom.
My Mom was the
youngest of three
children

This time line shows the history of Tim's family. The last picture shows Tim on his way to school.

1970   1980   1990   2000   present

1998

My grandmother held me when I was born.

Here I am on my first day in second grade!

Try the Skill

1 What happened in 1998?

2 In what year did Tim's great great grandparents move here?

3 **Activity** Make a time line of important events in your life.

2.1.2 Compare and contrast their daily lives with those of their parents, grandparents, and/or guardians.

Then and Now

Vocabulary

guardian

Life has changed over the years. Some of the ways people do things have changed too.

Tamika's ancestors lived in Nigeria, a country in Africa. They wore brightly colored loose shirts called *bubas*. The women wore a scarf called a *gele*.

Some of Tamika's ancestors moved to the United States. Here is a picture of her great grandparents. The women usually wore dresses.

Today Tamika and her family dress up to go to work and school. But sometimes they like to wear T-shirts and jeans and just have fun. Tamika's family enjoys being together just like her ancestors did long ago.

 How did Tamika's ancestors dress differently from the way her family dresses today?

Chores Then and Now

Like families long ago, people today have chores they must do. Katia learned about her **guardian's** ancestors. A guardian is a person who takes care of you like a parent.

Katia's guardian had a grandmother who lived on a farm. Her grandmother had many chores to do. One chore was to go to the barn to gather eggs.

When Katia's guardian was a little girl, she had chores too. A milkman delivered eggs and milk to her home. Katia's guardian carried in the milk and eggs and put them away.

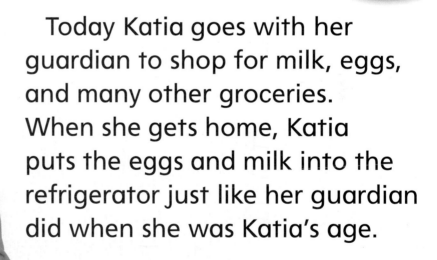

Today Katia goes with her guardian to shop for milk, eggs, and many other groceries. When she gets home, Katia puts the eggs and milk into the refrigerator just like her guardian did when she was Katia's age.

How do grocery stores make chores easier than they were long ago?

Games Then and Now

Josh went to a special museum where people showed him how to play hoop 'n' stick. His ancestors played this game a long time ago. They would roll the hoop along the ground. They pushed the hoop with a stick so it would not fall down.

Josh asked his uncle what games he played as a boy. Josh's uncle told him how he played Hula Hoop.

Today Josh plays with a coaster flying ring. It is easy to throw and catch because there is a hole in the middle. Josh and his friends play to see who can throw it the farthest.

 What do all these games have in common?

Lesson Review

1. What is a guardian?

Big Idea 2. Why is it important to learn about our ancestors?

3. **Compare and Contrast** How is your life today different than the life of your parent or guardian long ago?

Use Calendars

A **calendar** is a chart that shows the 12 months of the year. It also shows the number of days in each month and the seven days of the week. Calendars remind us of places we have to go and things we need to do.

Look at the calendar on the next page. It is for the month of September. Find the number 4. September 4 is on a Monday. What holiday is on that day?

Try the Skill

1. What day of the week is Grandparents Day?
2. How many days long is the School Bake Sale?
3. **Activity** Make a special calendar for your birthday month.

September

Sunday	Monday	Tuesday	Wednesday	Thursday	Friday	Saturday
					1	2
3	4 Labor Day Family Picnic	5	6	7	8	9 Play catch with Pedro
10 Grandparents Day	11	12	13	14 Do chores	15	16
17	18	19 School Bake Sale	20 School Bake Sale	21	22	23 First Day of Fall
24	25	26	27	28 Do chores	29	30

2.1 Students differentiate between things that happened long ago and things that happened yesterday.

America's Families Long, Long Ago

Vocabulary

Native American

settler

mission

Pilgrim

Native Americans were the first people to live in America. They are also called American Indians. There were many different groups of American Indians.

Plains Indians hunted buffalo. They built movable homes, called teepees, out of wooden poles and buffalo skin. When the buffalo left the area, they could pick up their homes and follow.

Pueblo Indian families grew beans, corn, and squash. They used ladders to reach the doors of their homes!

The Pacific Northwest Indians were great fishers. They carved and painted large totem poles that told about their lives.

 Why was it important for the Plains Indians to have movable homes?

Spanish Families Arrive

For a long time Native Americans were the only people to live here. Then Spanish **settlers** arrived. A settler is a person who moves from one place to live in another place. The Native Americans showed them how to grow food like corn, potatoes, and squash.

The first Spanish settlers built a town called St. Augustine. Today St. Augustine is in the state of Florida.

Spanish settlers build St. Augustine.

Mission St. Augustine

40

Father Junipero Serra was a priest from Spain. He started many **missions** in California. A mission is a place where a group of church members live and work. Native Americans were forced to work hard building the missions. But the missions were the beginning of many important California cities, like San Diego, Los Angeles, and San Francisco.

Father Junipero Serra

 What is St. Augustine?

Mission San Juan Capistrano

Mission San Diego

The Pilgrims Arrive

The **Pilgrims** were a group of people from England who traveled to America. They sailed on a ship called the *Mayflower*.

Statue of Squanto

The Pilgrims had a hard winter. They did not know how to live in their new home. One Native American named Squanto had once lived in England. He knew how to speak English. He showed the Pilgrims how to fish, hunt, and grow food.

The Pilgrims arrive in America.

By fall the Pilgrims had lots of food. They made a big meal. Squanto and other Native Americans joined the Pilgrims for the special meal. The Pilgrims thanked God for all the good things that had happened. Every year we celebrate this event on Thanksgiving Day.

How did Squanto help the Pilgrims?

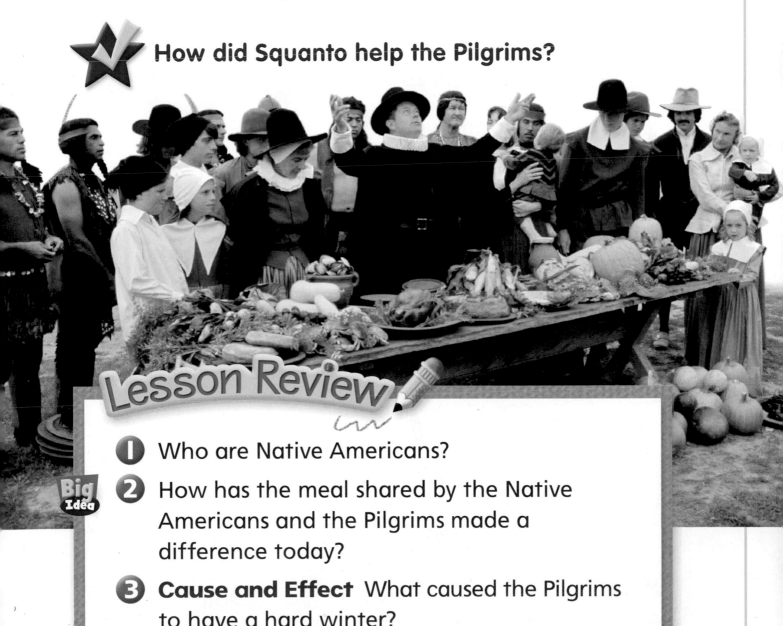

Lesson Review

1. Who are Native Americans?

Big Idea 2. How has the meal shared by the Native Americans and the Pilgrims made a difference today?

3. **Cause and Effect** What caused the Pilgrims to have a hard winter?

2.1

A Thanksgiving Story

Characters

Hope, a Pilgrim woman • **Miles,** a Pilgrim man
• **Squanto,** a Native American man
• **Aponi,** a Native American woman

Narrator: It is December 16, 1620 in Plymouth, Massachusetts. The *Mayflower* has just arrived. The Pilgrims get off the ship.

Hope: Where will we live? It is so cold here!

Miles: We must begin to build houses at once. There is no time to lose. Winter is already here.

Narrator: It was a cold and hard winter. Many Pilgrims got sick. They did not have enough food. Then one day there was a knock on their door.

Squanto: We came to help you. I am Squanto. This is my friend Aponi.

Hope: We do not have enough to eat. We are so hungry.

Aponi: Squanto can help you. He can show you how to plant and hunt and fish.

Narrator: That is just what Squanto did. Squanto showed the Pilgrims how to plant corn.

Squanto: First place a dead fish in the soil.

Hope and Miles: A dead fish?

Aponi: It will make the soil rich. Then you will have lots of corn.

Narrator: When summer came the Pilgrims had a lot of food. They stored food for the winter.

Hope: The harvest has been good. We will not be hungry this winter.

Miles: We will have a feast to give thanks to God for our harvest and our new Native American friends.

Narrator: Miles and Hope walk over to Aponi and Squanto's home.

Squanto: Hello, my friends.

Aponi: How can we help you now?

Miles: We want to invite you and your family and friends to a special meal.

Hope: It is a meal of thanksgiving. We are thankful for friends like you.

Miles: You have saved our lives.

Narrator: The Native American and the Pilgrim families celebrated together for three days. Today we still celebrate Thanksgiving. We give thanks for all that we have.

Write About It! Make a list of five things you are thankful for.

Use Map Scales

Look at the map of St. Augustine, Florida, on the next page. It has a **map scale**. A map scale tells the distance between places on a map. On this map the map scale shows that one inch equals 100 miles. Follow the steps to use the map scale.

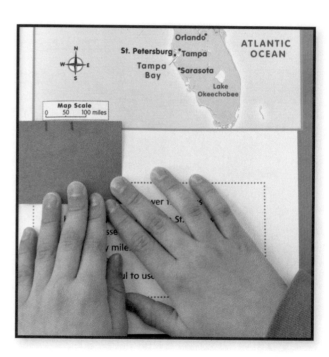

1 Place a strip of paper between St. Augustine and Gainesville. First draw a mark where St. Augustine is on the strip of paper. Then mark where Gainesville is.

2 Place the strip of paper on the map scale. Put one of the marks at zero. What number does the second mark come closest to? Do you see that St. Augustine and Gainesville are about 50 miles apart?

St. Augustine, Florida

★Tallahassee   • Jacksonville

     • ST. AUGUSTINE

Gainesville•

Gulf of Mexico

Orlando•

St. Petersburg• •Tampa

Tampa Bay

•Sarasota

Lake Okeechobee

ATLANTIC OCEAN

N W E S

Map Scale
0   50   100 miles

Try the Skill

Mark paper strips to answer the questions.

1 How many miles is it from St. Augustine to Tallahassee?

2 How many miles is it from St. Petersburg to Orlando?

3 Why is a map scale useful?

5

Families on the Move

Vocabulary

pioneer

immigrant

More and more people came to cities in the East. Families began to move West to make new homes. We call these people **pioneers**. Pioneers are people who leave their homes to lead the way into a land they do not know.

It was very hard for pioneer families to travel with no roads or signs. Often they or their horses got sick. Some pioneers had little food. It took months for families to drive their covered wagons across rivers and mountains.

Life on the trail was filled with danger. Sometimes pioneers got lost or hurt. Pioneers and their horses were worn out at the end of their long journey.

 **Why was it hard for the pioneers to travel West?**

Native American Families Move

Some Native Americans shared their land with the pioneers. The Eastern Woodland Indians in Rhode Island lived peacefully with the pioneers.

Most Native American families were forced to leave their land. This was because the United States government wanted to make room for the pioneers. The Cherokee Indians lived in Georgia. American soldiers forced them to leave their land. The Cherokee were made to walk or ride horses to what is now the state of Oklahoma.

The Cherokee are forced to leave.

The Trail of Tears

It took the Cherokee Indians a year to arrive in Oklahoma. In their own language the Cherokee called this walk "the place where they cried." Later it became known as the Trail of Tears.

Why do you think the Cherokee called their walk "the place where they cried"?

Families Move by Sea

Many **immigrant** families also came to California. Immigrants are people who leave one country to live in another.

In the 1840s many people from Ireland sailed to New York on ships called *frigates.* They heard about gold in California. They wanted to find gold to make better lives for themselves.

In the 1850s Chinese immigrants sailed to Monterey, California, on large ships called *junks.*

A Chinese junk

Frigate arriving in New York

Many Chinese immigrants came to work on the railroads. They built the part of the railroad that went through the Sierra Nevada mountains.

What immigrant families did long ago makes a difference in our world today.

 Why did some people from Ireland come to California?

Lesson Review

1. Why did pioneers travel West?

Big Idea 2. What did the Chinese immigrants do that changed our lives today?

3. **Compare and Contrast** How were the Eastern Woodlands Indians and the Cherokee Indians alike? How were they different?

Use History Maps

A history map shows what places looked like a long time ago. The history map on the next page shows the path taken by the Cherokee Indians. It is called the Trail of Tears.

This map also shows the **borders** of the states as they are today. A border is a line that separates one state or country from another.

Try the Skill

1 Which rivers does the water path follow?

2 Which two paths pass through Memphis?

3 What does this map tell you about the past?

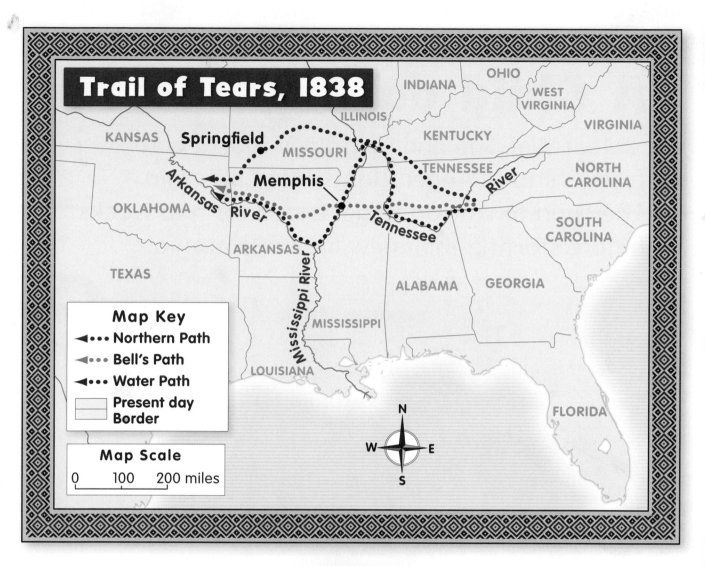

Trail of Tears, 1838

OHIO
INDIANA
WEST VIRGINIA
ILLINOIS
VIRGINIA
KANSAS
Springfield
MISSOURI
KENTUCKY
TENNESSEE
NORTH CAROLINA
Arkansas River
Memphis
River
OKLAHOMA
SOUTH CAROLINA
ARKANSAS
Tennessee
TEXAS
Mississippi River
ALABAMA
GEORGIA
MISSISSIPPI
LOUISIANA
FLORIDA

Map Key
◄••• Northern Path
◄••• Bell's Path
◄••• Water Path
▢ Present day Border

Map Scale
0   100   200 miles

N
W   E
S

A Child on Angel Island

Meet Wei. She and her family took a boat from China to Angel Island near California. They had to stay on Angel Island for two weeks before starting their new life in California.

▲ I eat both Chinese food and new American food with my family while we stay here on Angel Island.

◄ My mom helped me pack my suitcase in China before we left. I brought my clothes and toys with me.

◀ This is my favorite coat. I can not wait to wear it when we get to San Francisco!

My mom and dad are helping me learn to play chess. It makes our time here on Angel Island pass by more quickly. ▼

What things would you pack if you and your family moved to another country?

LOG ON

For more about life on Angel Island, visit:

www.macmillanmh.com/ss/ca/dayinthelife

2.1.1 Trace the history of a family through the use of primary and secondary sources, including artifacts, photographs, interviews, and documents.

America Grows

Vocabulary

culture

citizen

Many Asian immigrants sailed to Angel Island in California. Immigrants from Europe sailed to Ellis Island in New York. They could see the Statue of Liberty when they sailed into New York. The Statue of Liberty stands for freedom.

Ellis Island in New York

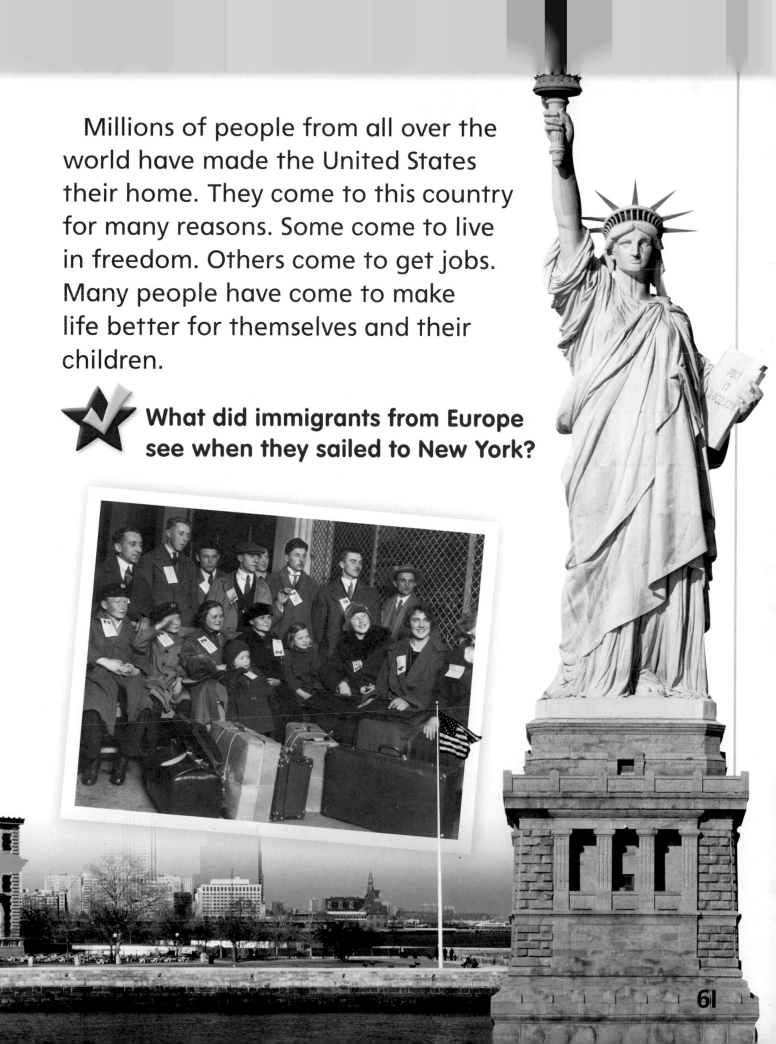

Millions of people from all over the world have made the United States their home. They come to this country for many reasons. Some come to live in freedom. Others come to get jobs. Many people have come to make life better for themselves and their children.

What did immigrants from Europe see when they sailed to New York?

The United States Today

Families have come to this country from all over the world. The United States is a country of immigrants. They brought many different **cultures** with them. Culture is the way a group of people live, including their food, music, and traditions. For example, yoga comes the culture of India. Eating with chopsticks comes from the culture of China.

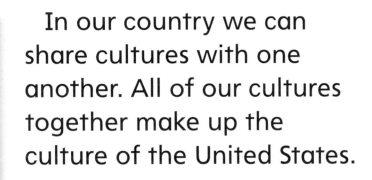

In our country we can share cultures with one another. All of our cultures together make up the culture of the United States.

People born in this country are called **citizens**. A citizen is a member of a community, state, or country. When immigrants come to the United States, they are not yet citizens. To become citizens they must first promise to make the United States their home and obey its laws. Many immigrants become citizens.

 What promise do immigrants make to become citizens of the United States?

Lesson Review

1. What is a citizen?

Big Idea 2. How have other cultures made a difference in our world today?

3. **Make Predictions** Predict what life would be like if we did not have freedom.

Keeping History Alive

Mrs. Talbert's class at J. H. Gunn School in Charlotte, North Carolina, heard some surprising news. Their old brick school building would soon be torn down. A new school would be built. Kristen Hargis says, "We all felt sad. We liked our school."

"We decided to make a video of our school and of the people who had gone there," says Ira Grier. "My grandma went to our school just like me!"

Ira's grandma and other students from the past visited the class. The children interviewed them while the teacher made a video. The video will be kept in the library of the new school. That way everyone can watch it and remember the old school.

 What are some ways you could help remember people or places?

Ira's grandma

Being a Good Citizen ★ ★ ★

Find out about something that happened in your community. Make a book that can help to remember it.

Charlotte, North Carolina

65

A Family in Egypt

Egypt is a country on the continent of Africa. Egypt is also very close to the continent of Asia. The cultures and traditions of Egyptian families come from both Africa and Asia.

Long ago families in Egypt wore loose fitting robes with hoods called *djellabas*. Djellabas are from Africa. Many families ate a pasta dinner called *koshary*. Koshary is from Asia.

An Egyptian family at dinner, about 100 years ago

Today Egyptian families eat foods and dress in clothing from all over the world. But they also might wear djellabas and eat koshary just like their ancestors did!

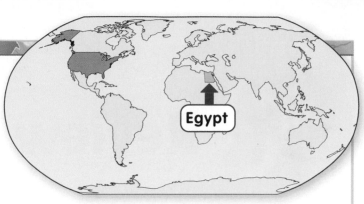

Egypt

An Egyptian family today

Write About It! What kind of clothing did your ancestors wear?

Review

Reading Social Studies

Compare and Contrast

Look at the pictures below. Then answer the questions.

1 Compare these two pictures. How are they alike?

2 Contrast these two pictures. How are they different?

The Golden Gate Bridge being built long ago

The Golden Gate Bridge today

Vocabulary

Use these words to finish the sentences.

mission   culture   interview

3 The way a group of people live, including their food, music, and traditions, is called _____.

4 A person asks another person questions and writes down the answers during an _____.

5 A _____ is a place where a group of church members live and work.

Critical Thinking

6 Why is passing down family traditions important?

7 Why do people settle in new lands?

8 List two things you use, do, or eat that came from another culture.

2.1.3

Chart and Graph Skills **Use Time Lines**

This time line shows the history of Li's family.

Li's family

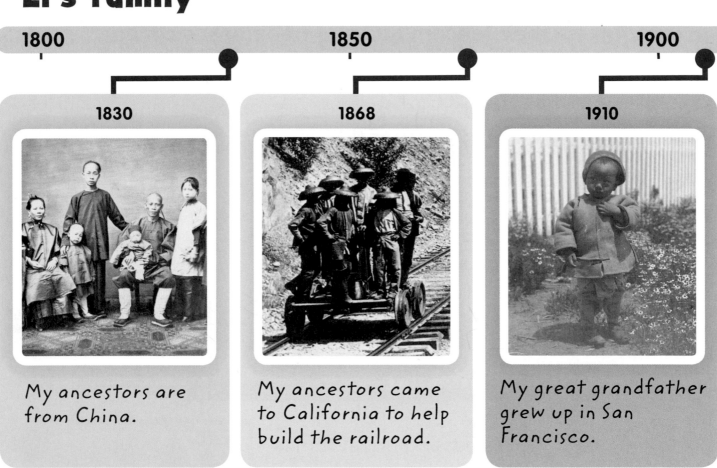

1800   1850   1900

1830
My ancestors are from China.

1868
My ancestors came to California to help build the railroad.

1910
My great grandfather grew up in San Francisco.

① Which event happened next after 1830?

A   Li's ancestors lived in China.

B   Li's grandparents got married.

C   Li's mother grew up in Los Angeles.

D   Li's ancestors helped build the railroad.

1950

2000

1960

My grandparents got married in 1960.

1970

This is my mom growing up in Los Angeles.

Today

My family and me living in Fresno.

2 Which event happened in 1960?

A Li's grandparents got married.

B Li's mother grew up in Los Angeles.

C Li's ancestors lived in China.

D Li's great grandfather grew up in San Francisco.

The **Big** Idea Activity

Ancestor Puppet

1. Write a paragraph telling how an ancestor made a difference in your life today.

2. Make a sock puppet of the ancestor. Use buttons, yarn, glue, or other things you can find.

3. Use your ancestor puppet to read your paragraph about him or her to others.

Read More About the Big Idea

To learn more about families from long ago, you can read one of these books.

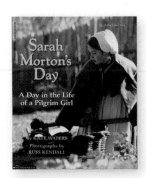

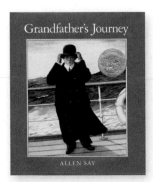

For help with the Big Idea activity, visit: www.macmillanmh.com/ss/ca/launchpad

UNIT

2

2.2 Students demonstrate map skills by describing the absolute and relative locations of people, places, and environments.

Exploring Our Earth

Explore
The Big Idea

How can we find out about places on Earth?

Canoeing on Silver Lake, California

Explore The Big Idea

How can we find out about places on Earth?

The word **geography** comes from two word parts. The part "geo" means *Earth*. The part "graphy" means *to tell about* or *write*. Geography tells about the things that make up our Earth.

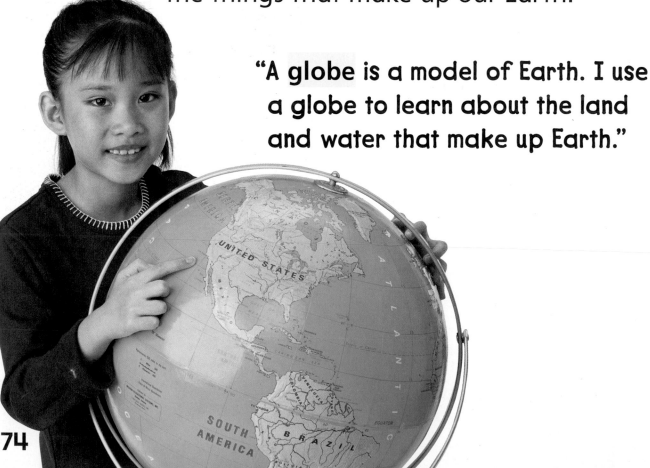

"A **globe** is a model of Earth. I use a globe to learn about the land and water that make up Earth."

"A map tells me how to find places."

"I can explore Earth. I can look at things in nature."

In this unit you will discover geography. You will find out about many places on Earth. You will learn how to use different kinds of maps.

Literature

The Treasure Hunt

by Becky Manfredini and Jenny Reznick
illustrated by Obadinah Heavner

It's time for a treasure hunt.
Here's what to do.
Follow the trail.
It's up to you!

Walk over two hills.
Walk onto flat land.
Now board the train.
I will give you a hand.

First take the train
to the water so blue.
Now ride in the boat.
Please row the boat, too!

Row and row
 until you see land.
Ahoy! There's the treasure.
It's on the gold sand!

Talk About It! How did the children travel along the trail?

Vocabulary
About Geography

Read the words in the boxes. Then look at the pictures.

An **urban** area is a city. (page 90)

A **suburban** area is an area near a city. (page 9l)

A **mountain** is the highest form of land. (page 98)

A **desert** is a hot, dry area with few plants. (page 99)

Write About It!

What do you see in these pictures?

81

Find the Main Idea and Details

The **main idea** tells what a paragraph is about. **Details** tell more about the main idea. Finding the main idea and details can help you understand and remember what you read.

Read the paragraph. Then try the skill.

Josh needed help finding things at his new school. The principal showed him where to find his new classroom. The teacher showed him where to sharpen his pencils. His new friend Anne showed him the playground behind the school.

To find the main idea and details,

- Read the paragraph.

- What sentence tells what the paragraph is about? That is the main idea.

- What sentences tell more about the main idea? Those are the details.

You can put your information in a web like the one shown below. One of the details has been filled in for you.

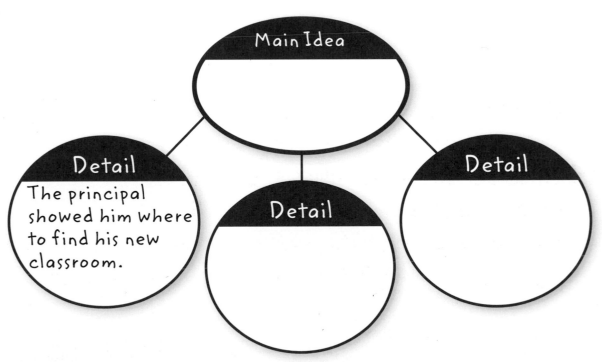

Main Idea

Detail

The principal showed him where to find his new classroom.

Detail

Detail

Try the Skill

1 What is the main idea of the paragraph?

2 Which other sentences give details?

3 Why is it helpful to find the main idea?

2.2 Students demonstrate map skills by describing the absolute and relative locations of people, places, and environments.

All About Location

Vocabulary

location

absolute location

relative location

Look at the things in this classroom photo. Each thing is in a certain place, or **location**. A location is the place or area where something is. The work table is located in the bottom right of the photo. The globe is located on the cubbies by the door.

Everything you see is in its own location. A location can be large or small. Your chair is in a location. Your school is in a location. You are in a location!

This is a map of the same classroom. Maps make it easy to see the location of things.

 Tell where you are located in your classroom.

Map Key

 Globe

 Table

 Rug

 Computer

 Cubbies

Map and Globe Skills

Where is the computer located?

Kinds of Locations

There are two kinds of locations. **Absolute location** tells the exact spot where something is. Your home address tells the absolute location of your house.

See the three houses on Elm Street below. Each address tells the absolute location of that home. You can see three absolute locations. They are 12 Elm Street, 13 Elm Street, and 14 Elm Street.

Relative location tells where something is by comparing it to another thing. You often use words like *near, far, next to, above,* and *below* when telling the relative location of something.

For example, the blue house is *next to* the red house. We can tell the location of the blue house by comparing it to the red house. This tells the relative location of the blue house.

How could you use relative location to help a new child find things in your school?

Lesson Review

1. What is the relative location of the street sign to the blue mailbox?

Big Idea 2. Tell the absolute location of where you live.

3. **Find the Main Idea and Details** What is the main idea of this lesson?

Use Grid Maps

The map on the next page is called a **grid map**. A grid map is divided by lines. The lines form squares. A letter and a number give the name for each square.

The letters are on the left and right sides of the map. The numbers are on the top and bottom. This makes the map easier to use.

Put your finger on the first square in the top row. The square is A1. The school is in square A1. Now move your finger down three squares to square D1.

···· Try the Skill ····

1 What is in square D1?

2 Find the library. What square is it in on the grid map?

3 **Activity** Make a grid map of your classroom, school, or community.

Neighborhood Grid Map

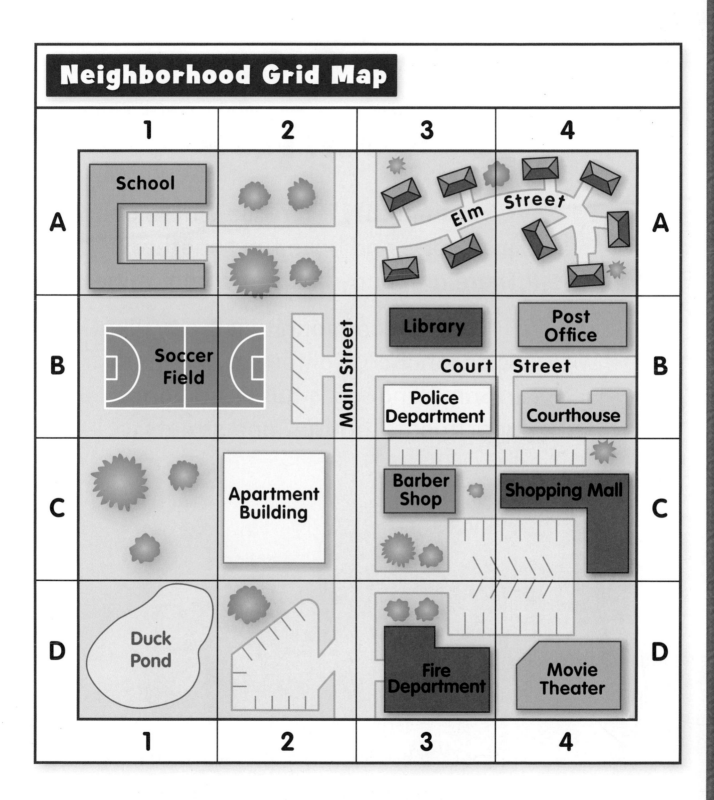

From City to Country

Vocabulary

community

urban

suburban

rural

A **community** is a place where people live, work, and have fun together. There are many kinds of communities.

An **urban** community is a city, like San Francisco, California. The land in San Francisco is full of buildings, apartments, houses, and streets.

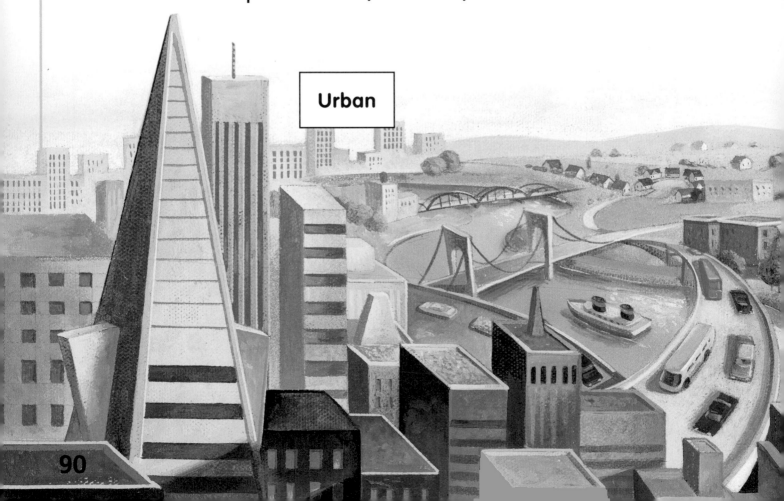

Urban

A **suburban** community is an area near a city. The word suburb is made out of two word parts. The part "sub" means *near* and the part "urb" means *city*. Many people who live in a suburban community go to work in the nearby city.

A **rural** community is located far away from a city. Rural means open land. There is a lot of land, but only a few houses in a rural community.

 Tell the relative location of a suburban community.

Suburban

Rural

Using the Land

The most crowded part of an urban community is called downtown. You will find the tallest buildings downtown. Many people work in these buildings.

San Francisco is an urban area.

A suburban community has more open areas, like parks and fields. Every day more people move to live in suburban areas. Many work in the nearby city. They often get stuck in traffic when driving to work.

Burlingame is a suburban area.

Rural communities are made up of small towns, farms, and lots of land. Many farms grow fruits and vegetables.

How is land used in an urban community?

Napa is a rural area.

How People Live in a Community

In urban communities, or cities, people live close together. Many people live in apartment buildings and do not need a car to get around. There are lots of things close by to see and do.

In suburban communities people often drive to a shopping mall or a movie theater. They can play games outside or have a family barbecue in their yard.

In rural areas there is lots of land. There is plenty of room to play or have a picnic outdoors! Most people live in houses. Some drive to the nearby town to shop or meet friends.

 What can people do to have fun in a rural community?

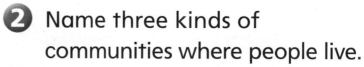
Lesson Review

Big Idea

1. What is a community?
2. Name three kinds of communities where people live.
3. **Compare and Contrast** How are an urban and suburban community alike? Different?

Use Bar Graphs

A **bar graph** is a graph that uses bars to show and compare information.

This bar graph shows how many inches of rain usually fall in San Francisco each winter, spring, summer, and fall.

Move your finger up the bar for spring. It ends at the number 5. That means San Francisco has about 5 inches of rainfall in the spring.

Try the Skill

1 What other time does San Francisco have 5 inches of rainfall?

2 When does San Francisco have the most rainfall?

3 **Activity** Make your own bar graph of weather in your community.

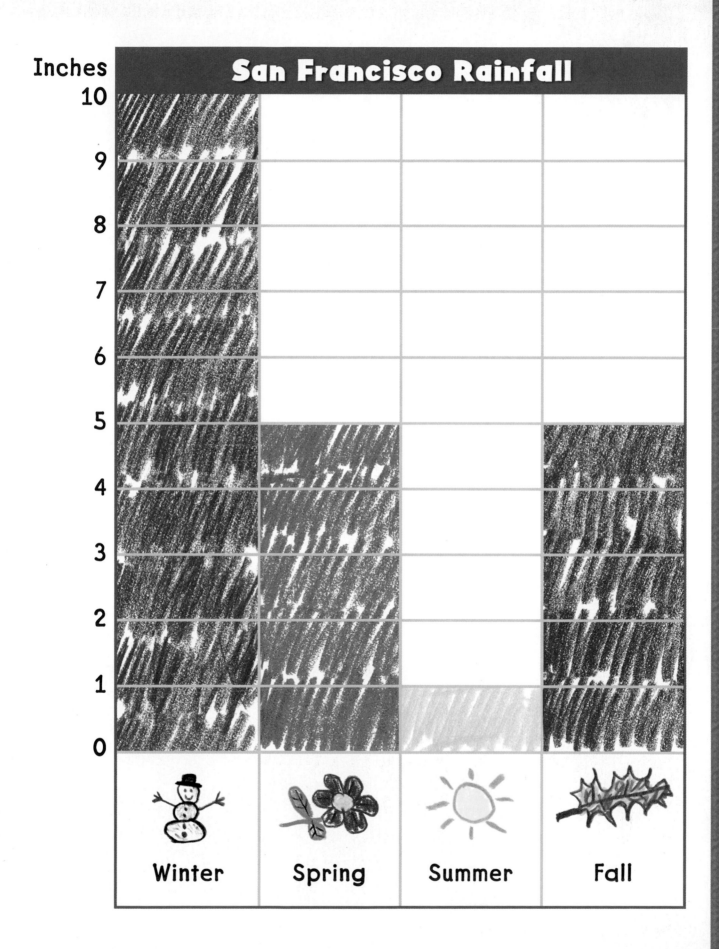

San Francisco Rainfall

Inches

Winter | Spring | Summer | Fall

97

3

Land and Water

Vocabulary

landform

mountain

hill

valley

plain

desert

ocean

island

peninsula

coast

river

lake

Emily and her family took a trip through California. They saw many different kinds of land and water.

The different shapes of land on Earth are called **landforms**. A **mountain** is the highest form of land. A **hill** is higher than the land around it, but not as high as a mountain.

We started our trip at Mount Shasta near my home in Redding, California.

Emily's family visited a mountain near her home. Then they drove south through a **valley**. A valley is the low area between mountains or hills. Some land is flat. Flat land is called a **plain**.

Then Emily's family came to a place with sand and rocks. It was a **desert**. A desert is dry and hot. It has fewer plants than other landforms.

What landforms did Emily see?

There were lots of poppies growing on this plain.

It sure was hot in the desert!

We drove through part of Yosemite Valley.

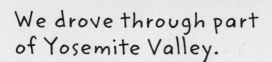

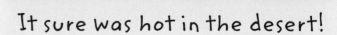

99

Landforms Near Water

Emily's family left the desert and drove to the **ocean**. An ocean is the largest body of water. The water in the ocean is salt water. Salt water is not good to drink. It can make you sick!

The Pacific Ocean runs along the west side of California.

We went swimming and fishing on Catalina Island.

At the ocean they saw more landforms. The first landform had water going all the way around it. It is called an **island**. Emily's family rode a boat to Catalina Island.

After they left the island they drove north to Monterey, California. Monterey is a **peninsula**. A peninsula is a landform that has water on all sides but one.

When Emily's family left Monterey Peninsula, they drove along the **coast**. A coast is land that runs along the water.

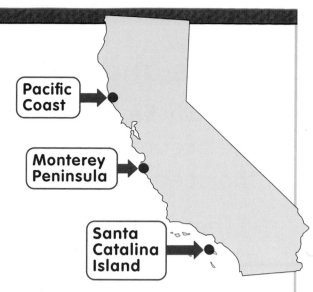

This coast runs along the Pacific Ocean.

 How are a peninsula and an island different?

We fed gulls on Monterey Peninsula.

Lakes and Rivers

Finally Emily's family drove away from the ocean. Emily soon found out that the ocean is not the only body of water!

They stopped to see the beautiful Klamath **River**. A river is a single stream of water that flows into a larger body of water, like an ocean. A river is always made of fresh water. There is no salt in fresh water.

Lake Shasta is near my home in Redding, California.

The Klamath River runs through California and Oregon.

The last stop on the trip was **Lake** Shasta near Emily's home. A lake is a body of water. It is smaller than an ocean. It has land all around it. A lake can be made up of either salt water or fresh water.

Klamath River

Lake Shasta

Emily's family arrived home feeling tired, but happy. Emily took out her photos to look at all the places they had visited.

What two kinds of water can make up a lake?

Lesson Review

Big Idea

1. What landform is dry and hot?
2. What is the largest body of water?
3. **Compare and Contrast** How are an ocean, river, and lake alike? Different?

Use Landform Maps

There is a special map that shows water and landforms. It is called a landform map. Landform maps use colors to show different kinds of water and land.

Look at the pictures with the color squares on this page. What color stands for water? Mountains? Plains? Deserts? Now look at the landform map of California on the next page.

The map key shows the colors used for each kind of landform. Use the map and map key to answer the questions.

Blue shows water.

Orange shows mountains.

Green shows plains.

Yellow shows deserts.

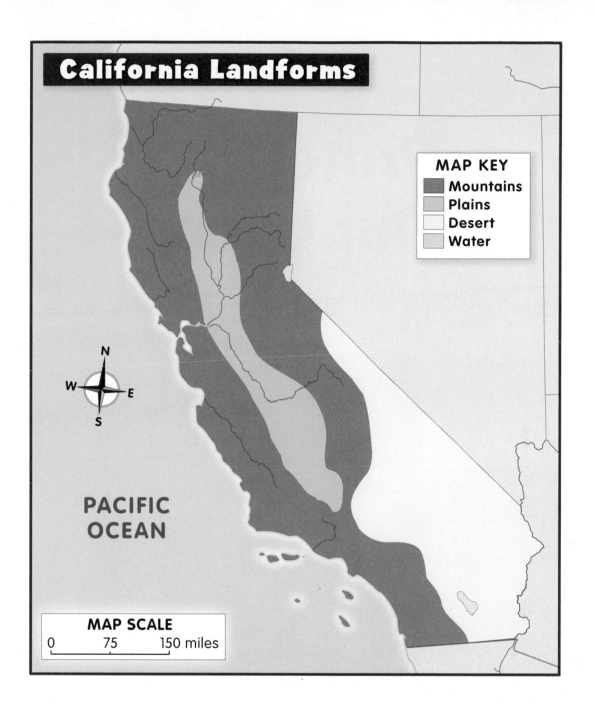

California Landforms

MAP KEY
- Mountains
- Plains
- Desert
- Water

N W E S

PACIFIC OCEAN

MAP SCALE
0   75   150 miles

Try the Skill

1. What landform runs through the center of California?

2. Does California have a larger area of desert or plains?

3. **Activity** Make your own landform map of California.

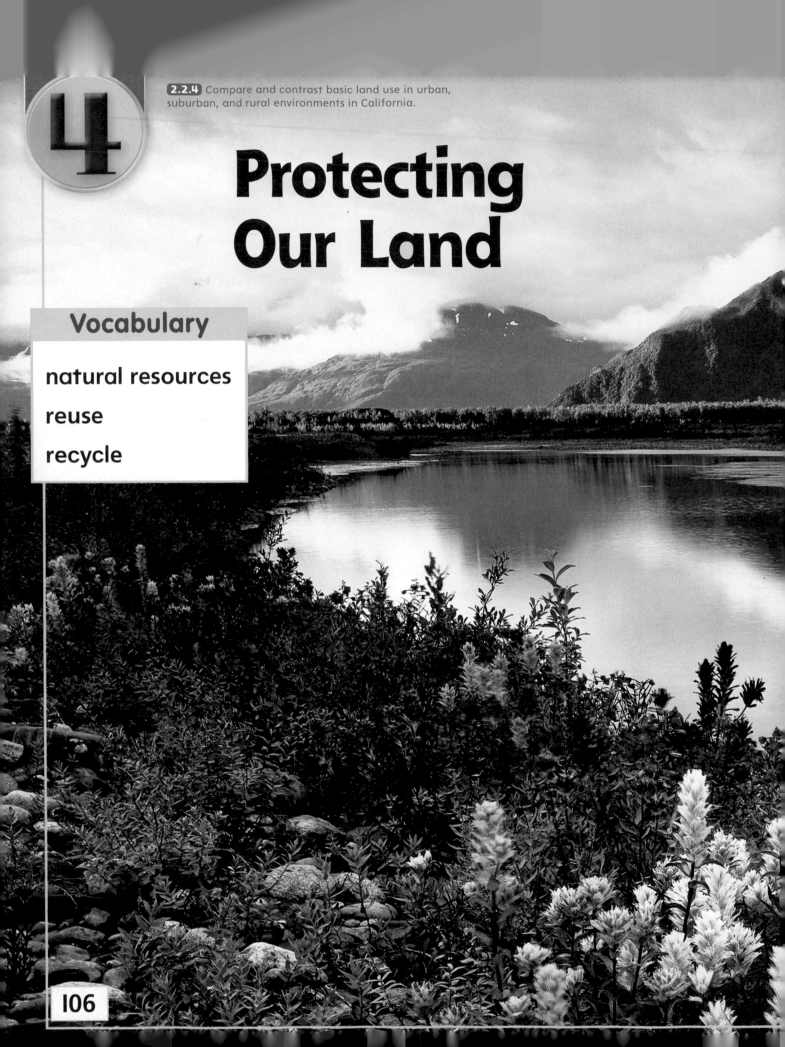

4

2.2.4 Compare and contrast basic land use in urban, suburban, and rural environments in California.

Protecting Our Land

Vocabulary

natural resources

reuse

recycle

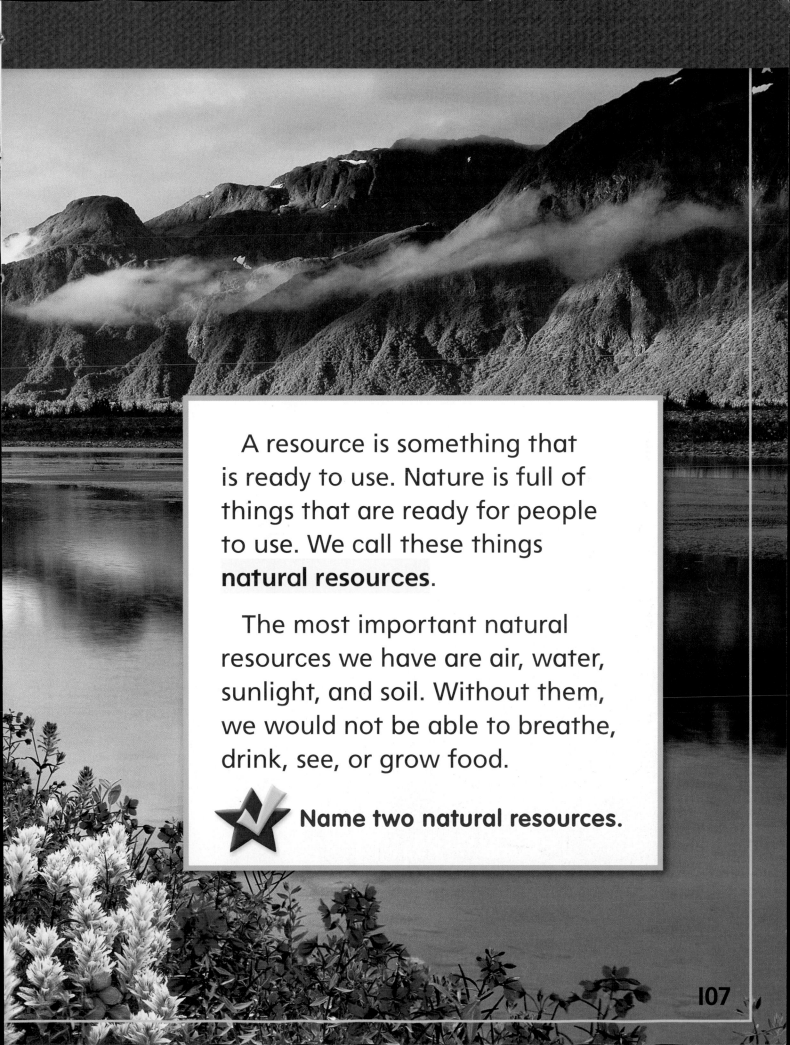

A resource is something that is ready to use. Nature is full of things that are ready for people to use. We call these things **natural resources**.

The most important natural resources we have are air, water, sunlight, and soil. Without them, we would not be able to breathe, drink, see, or grow food.

Name two natural resources.

Saving Our Trees

Our trees are an important natural resource. Trees are used to make many things like tables, chairs, and paper.

Sometimes forest fires help our forests by burning dead and dry plants. This makes room for new plants to grow. Other times forest fires burn out of control. When this happens the fire may burn down many of our trees.

A forest fire

People can help prevent unwanted forest fires. They can remove dead trees that cause many fires to spread. They can carefully put out campfires when they have finished using them.

We can plant new trees, but they take a long time to grow. If too many trees are burned or cut down, we might not have enough in the future.

How can forest fires be prevented?

Growing new trees

Putting out a campfire

109

Helping Earth

There are many ways to help Earth stay healthy. We can save our natural resources by using less water.

We can clean up our beaches on cleanup day. Trash makes the water and beaches unsafe.

We can **reuse** things we already have, like empty jars and boxes. Reuse means to use again.

Children help Earth by cleaning up our beaches.

We can **recycle** things made of glass, paper, and metal. Recycle means to change a thing into something new that can be used again. For example, old paper can be made into new paper. Look at the bar graph to see things recycled in Mrs. Cody's class.

 What things do you reuse?

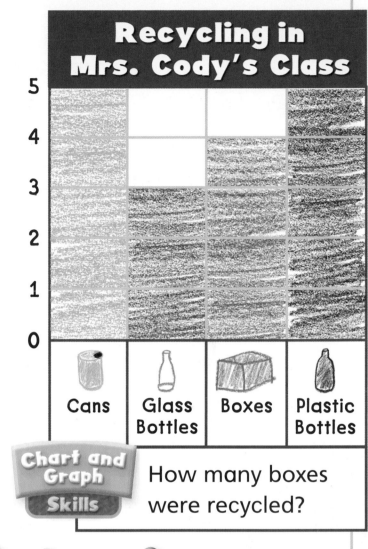

Recycling in Mrs. Cody's Class

| | 5 | 4 | 3 | 2 | 1 | 0 |

| Cans | Glass Bottles | Boxes | Plastic Bottles |

Chart and Graph Skills How many boxes were recycled?

Lesson Review

1. Why are air, water, sunlight, and soil our most important natural resources?

2. How can people help Earth stay healthy?

3. **Cause and Effect** What happens if we leave trash on the beach?

Big Idea

John Muir

John Muir cared about everything in nature. He spent his life writing, drawing, and speaking about it. Muir loved the Sierra Nevada mountains so much that he formed a group called the Sierra Club to protect them.

His words made people care about Earth. Read what John Muir wrote about how all things in nature work together.

Using Primary Sources

66 **When one tugs at a single thing in nature, he finds it attached to the rest of the world.** 99
— John Muir

Sierra Nevada Mountains

Once John Muir went on a camping trip with President Theodore Roosevelt. He told the President how he felt about protecting nature. After the trip President Roosevelt helped change millions of acres of forests into public parks.

What things did John Muir do to show he cared about nature?

Drawing by John Muir

Theodore Roosevelt and John Muir

LOG ON For more about John Muir, visit:

www.macmillanmh.com/ss/ca/bios

Respecting Nature

John Muir showed respect for nature. We show respect whenever we decide to honor other people, places, or things. We respect nature by caring about the living things on Earth.

Oh, look at the bird eggs, Anne! They are so cute. Let's take them home.

No, we should not do that, Marie. The baby birds cannot hatch if we take the eggs away.

Oh, you are right. We must leave them alone.

Look at the story. Find out what happened when Anne and Marie found a nest of eggs.

What did Anne and Marie decide to do about the bird eggs? Did they show respect for nature? What would you do if you found a nest with bird eggs?

Citizenship Activity

Make a poster showing one way you can respect living things in nature. Label your poster.

5

Our World

Vocabulary

state

country

continent

Meet Jamal. Jamal lives in the urban community of San Diego. San Diego is located in the **state** of California.

A state is part of a country. California is only one of the 50 states that make up our **country**. A country is the land and the people who live there. The name of our country is the United States of America.

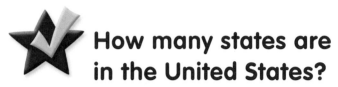 How many states are in the United States?

Our Country, Our Neighbors

Countries have neighbors. The countries of Mexico and Canada share a border with us. Mexico is our neighbor to the south. Canada is our neighbor to the north.

Together, the United States, its neighbors, and other countries form one large piece of land called a **continent**. The name of our continent is North America.

What two countries are neighbors of the United States?

UNITED STATES

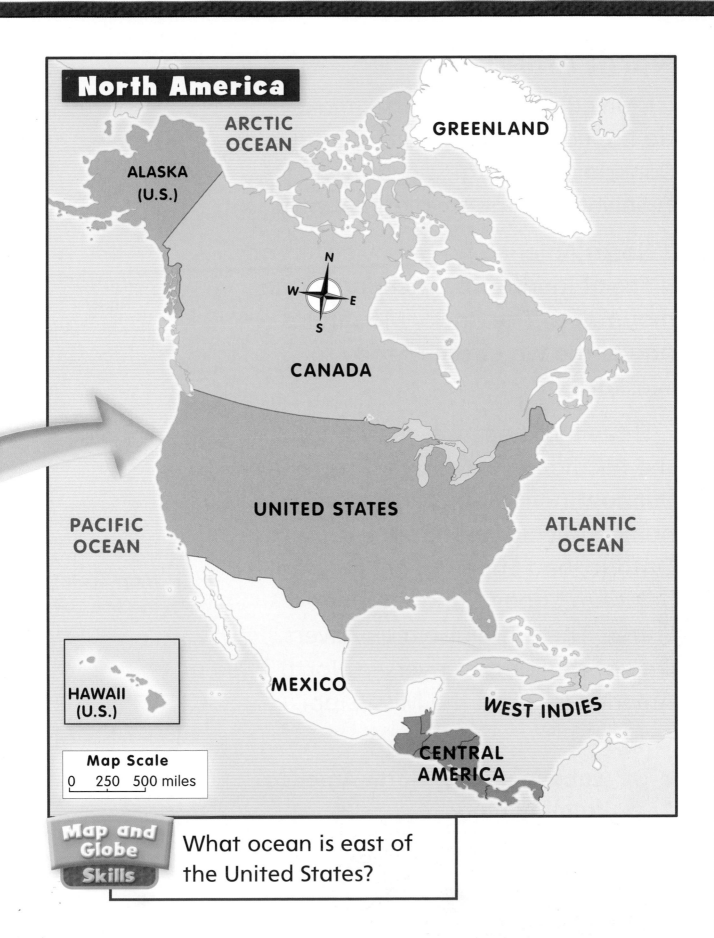

North America

ARCTIC OCEAN

GREENLAND

ALASKA (U.S.)

N
W   E
S

CANADA

UNITED STATES

PACIFIC OCEAN

ATLANTIC OCEAN

HAWAII (U.S.)

Map Scale
0   250   500 miles

MEXICO

WEST INDIES

CENTRAL AMERICA

Map and Globe Skills

What ocean is east of the United States?

North America

Many different countries make up the continent of North America. Canada is the largest country. El Salvador is the smallest country.

North America has many different kinds of landforms. There are huge mountains. The Rocky Mountains run all the way from Mexico to Alaska!

Three large oceans, the Atlantic, the Pacific, and the Arctic, surround our continent. Five Great Lakes, named Michigan, Huron, Erie, Ontario, and Superior, are located between Canada and the United States. There are also many rivers. One of the longest rivers in North America is called the Mississippi.

 Label a map of North America from memory.

| Title |

| Compass Rose |

| Map Scale |

| Map Key |

| Date |

North America

ARCTIC OCEAN

GREENLAND

ALASKA (U.S.)

PACIFIC OCEAN

R O C K Y   M O U N T A I N S

CANADA

Lake Superior
Lake Huron
Lake Ontario
Lake Michigan

SIERRA NEVADA MOUNTAINS

Missouri River

Mississippi River

Lake Erie

Ohio River

APPALACHIAN MOUNTAINS

Colorado River

UNITED STATES

ATLANTIC OCEAN

HAWAII (U.S.)

SIERRA MADRE

MEXICO

CUBA

BELIZE
HONDURAS
GUATEMALA
NICARAGUA
EL SALVADOR
COSTA RICA
PANAMA

Map Scale
0   250   500 miles

Map Key
Great Lakes
Rivers
Mountains

Map made in 2007

Map and Globe Skills

What mountain range is on the east side of North America?

Our World

North America is only one of seven continents that make up our world. The other continents are Africa, Antarctica, Asia, Australia, Europe, and South America.

Can you find North America on the map?

NORTH AMERICA

PACIFIC OCEAN

ATLANTIC OCEAN

Equator

SOUTH AMERICA

The seven continents make up the land on Earth. The rest of Earth is made up of water. There is more water on Earth than there is land!

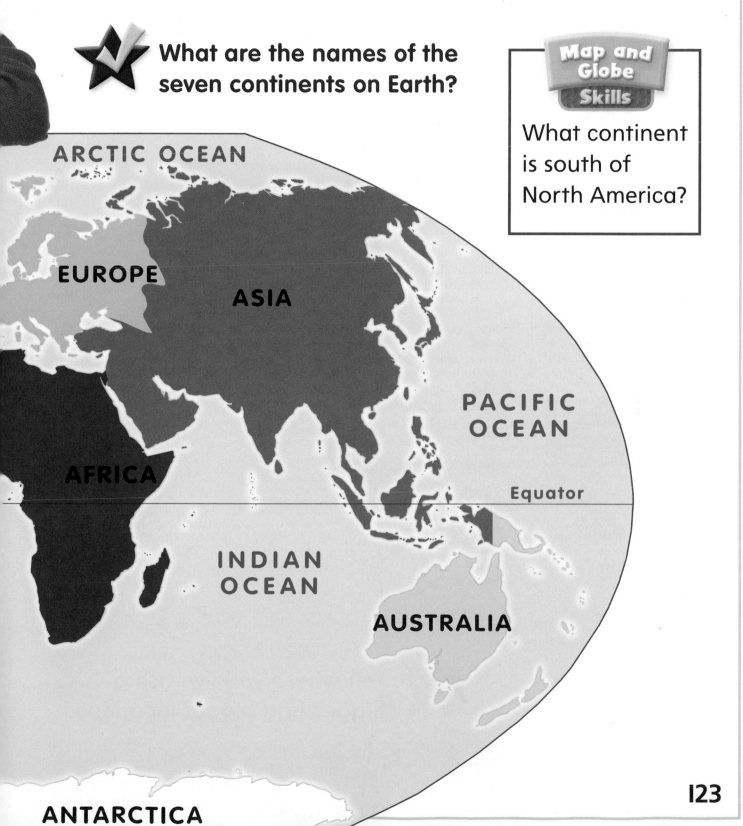

What are the names of the seven continents on Earth?

Map and Globe Skills

What continent is south of North America?

ARCTIC OCEAN

EUROPE

ASIA

AFRICA

PACIFIC OCEAN

Equator

INDIAN OCEAN

AUSTRALIA

ANTARCTICA

Our Location in the World

These pictures show where Jamal lives. It starts with his house and moves to bigger and bigger locations. All of these locations tell where Jamal lives.

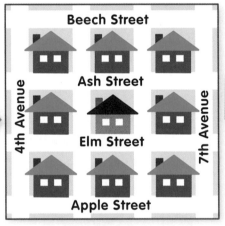

Jamal lives in a house.

Jamal's house is in the urban community of San Diego.

San Diego is in the state of California.

 Tell where you live using bigger and bigger locations.

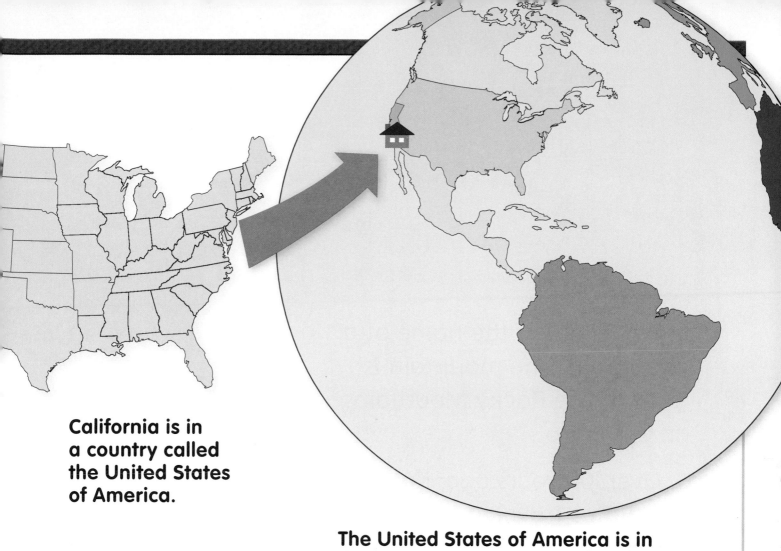

California is in a country called the United States of America.

The United States of America is in the continent of North America. North America is one of the seven continents on Earth.

1 What two things is Earth made of?

Big Idea 2 What is the largest location you learned about in this lesson?

3 **Find the Main Idea and Details** What is the main idea of this lesson?

125

Celebrate America's Beauty

2.2.2

with a Song

Pikes Peak is the name of a mountain. The mountain is part of the Rocky Mountains in Colorado.

Over 100 years ago, Katharine Lee Bates traveled to Pikes Peak. She said, "When I saw the view, I felt great joy." She wrote about what she saw. Her words became the song "America, the Beautiful."

America, the Beautiful

Words by Katharine Lee Bates

Music by Samuel Ward

O beau-ti-ful for spa-cious skies, For am-ber waves of grain.

For pur-ple moun-tain maj-es-ties, A - bove the fruit-ed plain.

A - mer - i - ca! A - mer - i - ca! God shed His grace on thee,

And crown thy good with broth-er-hood, From sea to shin-ing sea.

Activity

Draw a picture showing the things Katharine Lee Bates wrote about in "America, the Beautiful."

Pikes Peak

Did you know that today you can take a train to see the same beautiful view that Katharine Lee Bates saw more than 100 years ago?

1 **The train travels along a stream. There are large rocks that look like faces! You can see wildflowers, prairie dogs, and rabbits.**

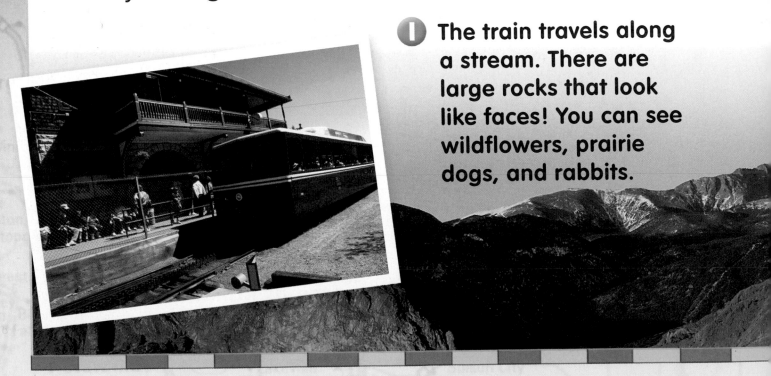

2 Close to the top, you will see many beautiful fir trees. You might see a mule deer or some bighorn sheep!

Pikes Peak, Colorado

COG RAILWAY

3 Finally the train stops at the top. It is 30 degrees colder here than it was at the bottom of the mountain! You can see the beautiful view all around you.

What kind of animals can you see on Pikes Peak?

LOG ON For more about Pikes Peak, visit:

www.macmillanmh.com/ss/ca/fieldtrips

2.2.3 Locate on a map where their ancestors live(d), telling when the family moved to the local community and how and why they made the trip.

The World Comes to California

Many groups of people have made California their home. The first people to arrive were Native Americans. They lived in four different landform areas of California. The four areas are coast, mountain, valley, and desert.

A Miwok basket

Some of these groups still live in California today. Two of these groups are the Miwok and the Yurok.

A Yurok family long ago

Long, long ago the Miwok and the Yurok lived on the coast next to the ocean. They learned how to be great fishers. The Yurok learned to make canoes from trees that grew along the coast. The Miwok made beautiful baskets from nearby plants.

Today the Miwok and Yurok still follow many of these traditions.

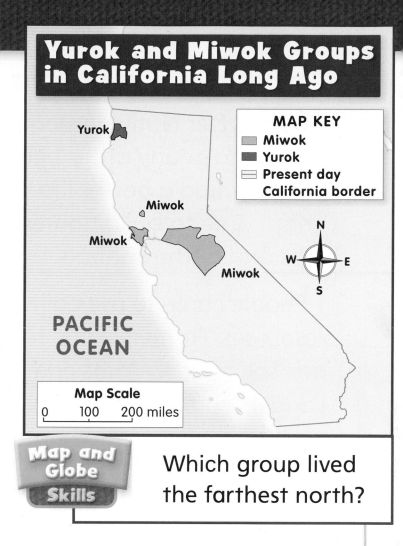

Yurok and Miwok Groups in California Long Ago

Yurok

Miwok

Miwok

Miwok

MAP KEY
- Miwok
- Yurok
- Present day California border

N W E S

PACIFIC OCEAN

Map Scale
0   100   200 miles

Map and Globe Skills

Which group lived the farthest north?

 Which two Native American groups lived along the coast?

A Yurok family today

Arriving in California

Long after Native Americans came to California, many other people came. They came to find a better life for their families. They came to build homes and find good jobs and better schools.

People came to use California's natural resources. Farmers came to use California's rich soil to grow fruits and vegetables. Loggers came to cut down trees. Fur traders and trappers came to hunt animals living in California's forests.

These immigrants came from Japan.

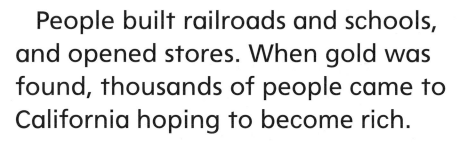

People built railroads and schools, and opened stores. When gold was found, thousands of people came to California hoping to become rich.

Years later people moved to California to build ships and airplanes, and to make movies. Today people still come from all over to make California their home.

What kind of work did people find in California?

This man is trying to find gold in California.

Our Ancestors

Our ancestors came to California from all over the world. They brought with them foods, celebrations, languages, and traditions from their countries.

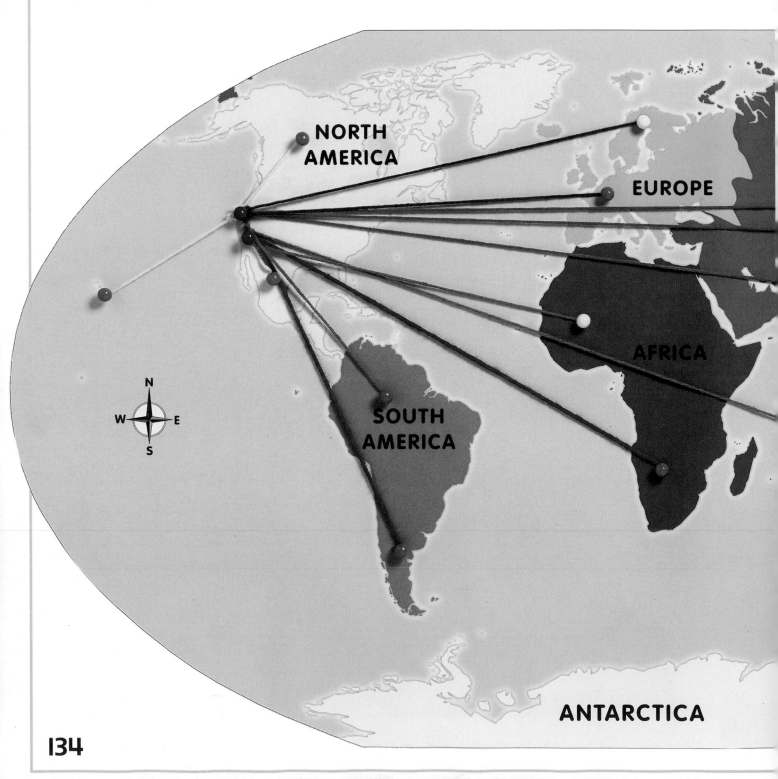

In California you can eat food from many cultures. You can celebrate different holidays and learn about places from all over the world. California's greatest treasure is its people!

What is one thing people have brought to California?

ASIA

AUSTRALIA

Lesson Review

Big Idea

1. Who were the first people to live in California?

2. From what continents have people come to California?

3. **Cause and Effect** What caused people to move to California?

Locate Information

Native American Art in California

Jane Smith

You can locate, or find, information in books. The **title** of a book can be found on its cover. The title is the name of the book. It tells you what the book is about. Look at this book title. It tells you this book is about different kinds of art by Native Americans in California.

The **table of contents** is in the front part of the book. It tells you the name of each chapter or lesson in the book. It also tells you on what page the chapter begins. Look at this table of contents from *Native American Art in California*. It shows that the name of Chapter I is "Baskets." It also shows that Chapter I begins on page 3.

Table of Contents

The name of the chapter can also be called the **chapter heading.** You can find the chapter heading on the first page of a chapter. This chapter heading can be found on page 3.

CHAPTER

1

Baskets

The Miwok Indians make beautiful baskets. The baskets are used for many different things. This basket is used to cook food.

Try the Skill

1. If you wanted to know about Native American painting, would this book be helpful? How do you know?

2. Look at the table of contents. What chapter would tell you about Native American jewelry?

3. On what page number does the chapter begin?

Australia's Outback

Red desert

Australia is the smallest of the seven continents. It is both a continent and a country. Australia has many beautiful landforms.

Many large mountains stop the rain from falling over a large area of land. Australians call this area the Outback. The Australian Outback is dry and mostly made up of sandy red deserts.

Spinifex grass

Bearded dragon lizard

Ayer's Rock

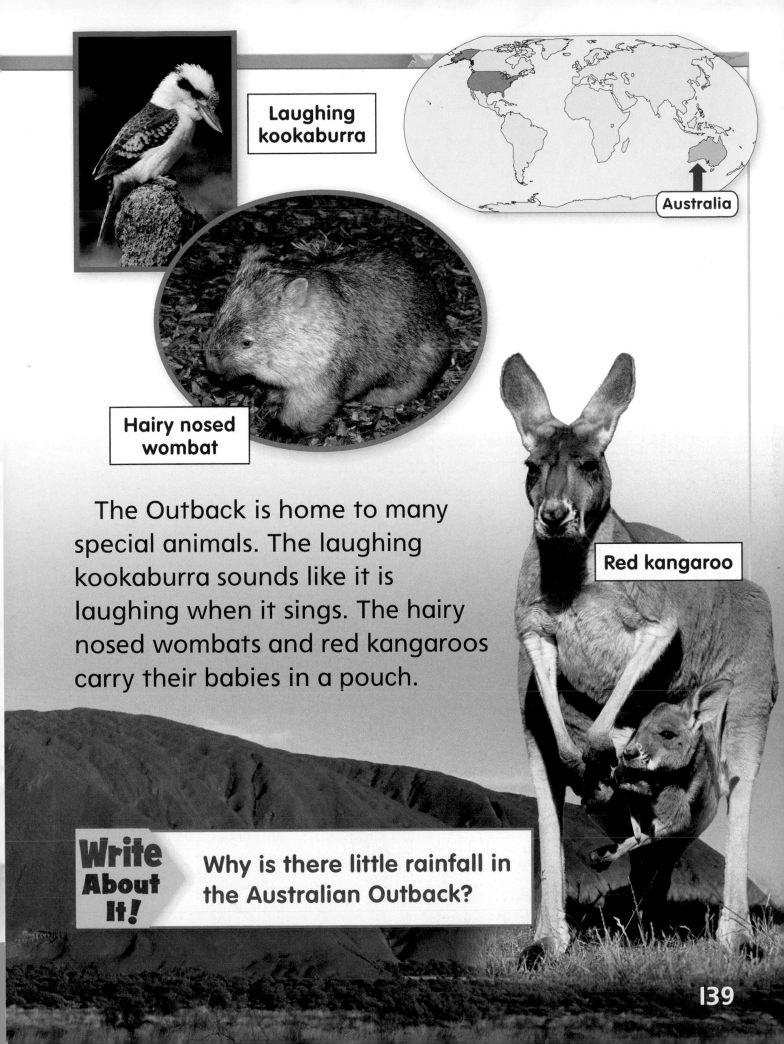

Laughing kookaburra

Australia

Hairy nosed wombat

Red kangaroo

The Outback is home to many special animals. The laughing kookaburra sounds like it is laughing when it sings. The hairy nosed wombats and red kangaroos carry their babies in a pouch.

Write About It!

Why is there little rainfall in the Australian Outback?

139

Reading
Social Studies

Find the Main Idea and Details

Read the paragraph. Then answer the questions.

Jeff is happy that his family moved to a rural community. He gets to ride a bus to school with other children who live too far away to walk. Now when his friend Jake visits, they have lots of space to play!

1. What sentence tells the main idea?

2. Which sentences tell the details?

Choose the word that best completes each sentence.

mountain   coast   recycled

3 The land that runs beside the ocean is called the _____.

4 The highest landform is a _____.

5 Old paper that is made into new paper is called _____ paper.

Critical Thinking

6 If you wanted to be in an area where there is lots of land, where would you go?

7 Why is it hard to grow food crops in a desert?

Write About It!

8 Write two sentences telling how Indians living on the coast of California used natural resources.

2.2.1

Map and Globe Skills **Use Grid Maps**

Look at the grid map below. Then answer the questions.

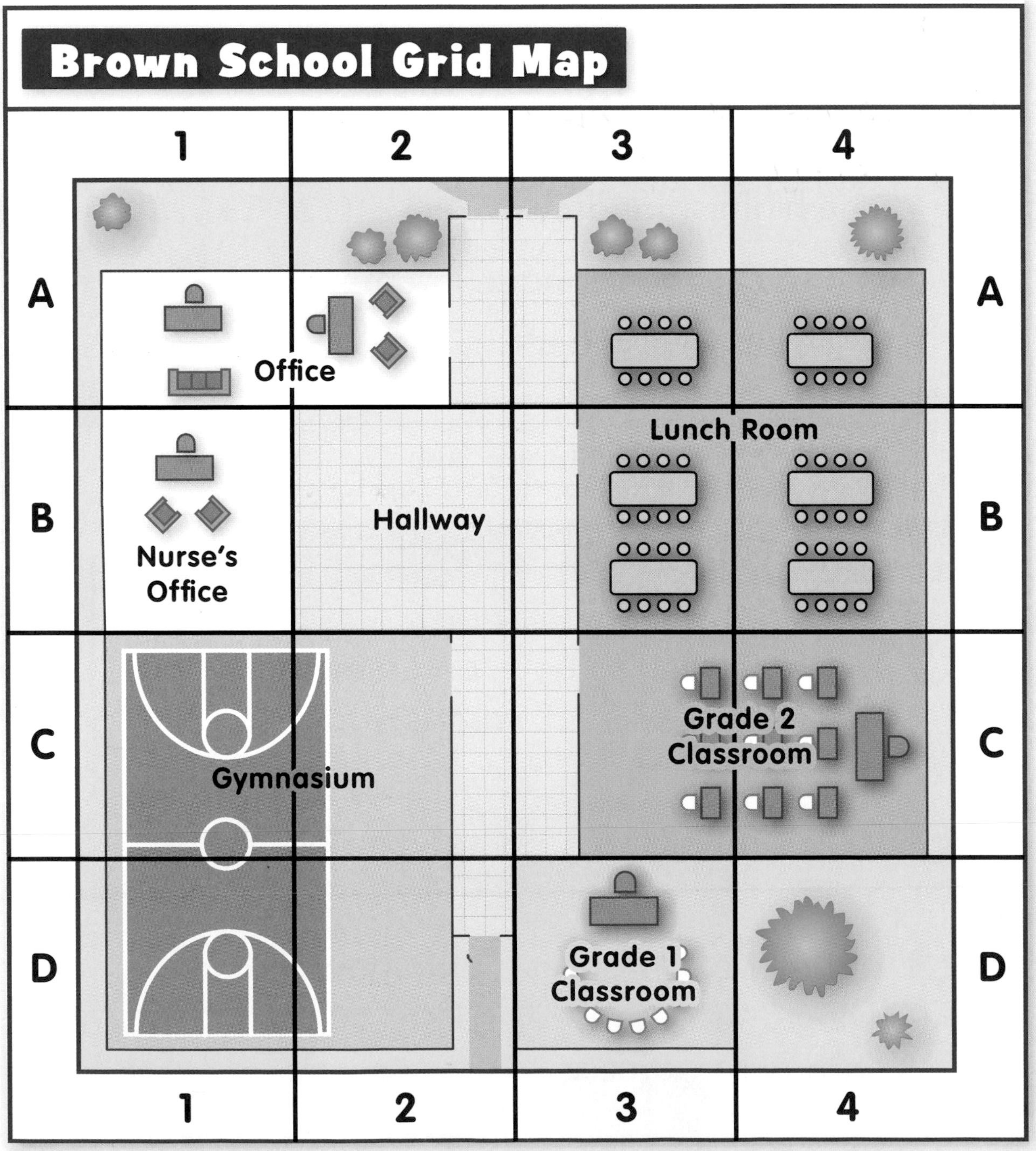

Brown School Grid Map

	1	2	3	4	
A	Office		Lunch Room		**A**
B	Nurse's Office	Hallway			**B**
C	Gymnasium		Grade 2 Classroom		**C**
D			Grade 1 Classroom		**D**
	1	2	3	4	

1 The Nurse's Office is in square _____.

    A   Al

    B   A2

    C   Bl

    D   B2

2 What room is found in square D3?

    A   Grade I Classroom

    B   Office

    C   Gymnasium

    D   Nurse's Office

3 What room is both in squares C3 and C4?

    A   Nurse's Office

    B   Grade 2 Classroom

    C   Lunch Room

    D   Hallway

The Big Idea Activity

Explore My Community Book

1 Draw three pictures of places in your community. One picture should show people. One picture should show a landform. One picture should show animals.

2 Write under each picture. Tell what is in the picture.

3 Make a cover. Staple the pages and the cover together to make a book.

4 Share your book with your class.

Read More About the Big Idea

To find out more about places on Earth, you can read one of these books.

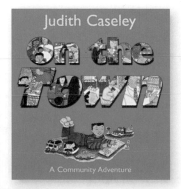

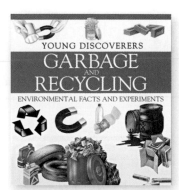

For help with the Big Idea activity, visit:

www.macmillanmh.com/ss/ca/launchpad

UNIT

3

2.3 Students explain governmental institutions and practices in the United States and other countries.

How Government Works

The Explore Big Idea

How does government help people get along?

Supreme Court building, Washington, D.C.

How does government help people get along?

Vocabulary

government

A **government** is the group of people who run a community, state, or country. Read about some of the ways government helps us get along.

"We believe that all people should be treated equally."

"Government workers meet to find ways to make our lives better."

"Our leaders work with leaders from other countries."

The citizens of our country choose the people who run our government. In this unit you will find out more about how our government works.

The Star-Spangled Banner

illustrated by Jill Newton

Words by Francis Scott Key

Music by John Stafford Smith

Oh, __ say! can you see, by the dawn's ear - ly light,

What so proud-ly we hailed at the twi-light's last gleam-ing?

Whose broad stripes and bright stars, through the per - il - ous fight,

O'er the ram-parts we watched were so gal-lant-ly stream-ing?

And the rock-ets' red glare, the bombs burst-ing in air,

Gave proof through the night that our flag was still there.

Oh, say, does that _ Star-Span-gled Ban-ner _ yet _ wave _

O'er the land ___ of the free and the home of the brave?

Talk About It! This song is about what symbol of our country?

Vocabulary
About Government

Read the words in the boxes. Then find the pictures in the big photographs.

The **Capitol** building is where our lawmakers work.
(page 171)

The **Supreme Court** is the most important court in our country.
(page 166)

The **President** is the leader of our country. (page 163)

The **White House** is where our President lives and works. (page 171)

Write About It! What do you see in these pictures?

Summarize

To **summarize** is to briefly tell or write about something you have read. When you summarize you include only the most important details.

To summarize,

- Read the paragraphs and look at any pictures.
- Find only the important details of the paragraphs.
- Briefly talk or write about the paragraphs.

You can put your information in a chart like the one shown below.

Summarize	
First Paragraph	Second Paragraph

Read the paragraphs. Then try the skill.

Mark's class made up some class rules. One rule is "Let eveyone have a turn."

They hung the list of rules on the wall. The new rules are helping everyone get along better.

1. Take turns.
2. Be polite.
3. Raise your hand before you speak.
4. Clean up your work area.
5. Listen to the teacher.

Try the Skill

1. What information do you need to summarize?
2. What details would you choose to summarize the paragraphs?
3. Why is it helpful to know how to summarize?

2.3.1 Explain how the United States and other countries make laws, carry out laws, determine whether laws have been violated, and punish wrongdoers.

Rules and Laws

Vocabulary

law

Constitution

vote

lawmaker

Rules are made to keep us safe, help us get along with each other, and keep things fair. Most classroom rules include "Clean up your work area" and "Raise your hand before you speak." These rules make the classroom a better place. What are some rules in your classroom?

A rule for a community or government is called a **law**. A law is a rule we must all follow. Wearing a helmet when you ride your bike is a law.

Why do we have rules and laws?

Our Constitution

Our country's first leaders knew that we needed to have laws to get along. They had a meeting. At this meeting they planned how our government would be run. They wrote out the plan on paper. They called this plan the **Constitution**.

The Constitution tells us how to run the government. It tells how we can make laws that help us get along with each other. It says that we are free to say what we think. It says that we are free to choose our religion.

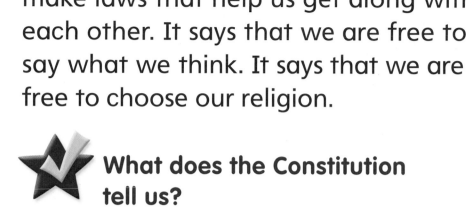 **What does the Constitution tell us?**

A Government by the People

The Constitution says that our government is run by its citizens. One way citizens do this is by **voting**. To vote is to choose someone or something. The person or thing with the most votes wins.

Citizens vote on new laws. But if *every* citizen voted on *every* new law, he or she would not have time to do other work! Our Constitution helps us with this problem.

Citizens voting

Waiting in line to vote

Our Constitution says that we can vote to choose a **lawmaker**. A lawmaker finds out what laws citizens want to have. Then he or she votes for these laws.

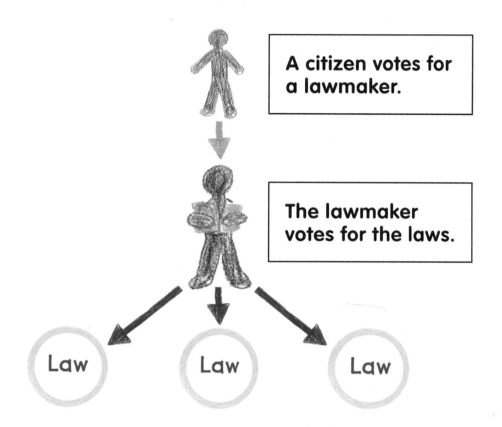

A citizen votes for a lawmaker.

The lawmaker votes for the laws.

Law   Law   Law

Name two ways that laws can be made.

Lesson Review

Big Idea

❶ What is the Constitution?

❷ What does a lawmaker do?

❸ **Summarize** Briefly tell or write how our government is run by its citizens.

Understanding Documents

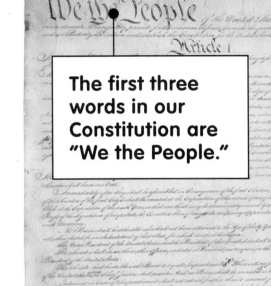

A **document** is a written or printed paper that gives information. A document can be a primary source. This document is the Constitution of the United States. It is four pages long.

The first three words in our Constitution are "We the People."

Look Closely

- The pages were written by hand long ago.
- The first three words tell us who runs our government.
- The last page was signed by state leaders.

George Washington

The LIBRARY of CONGRESS

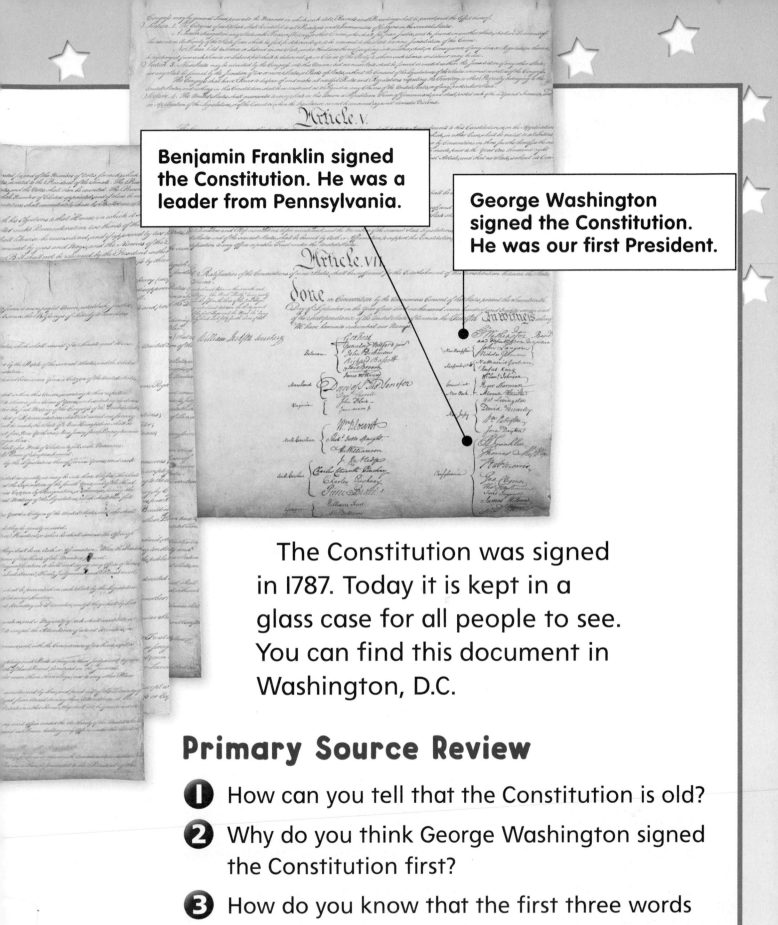

Benjamin Franklin signed the Constitution. He was a leader from Pennsylvania.

George Washington signed the Constitution. He was our first President.

The Constitution was signed in 1787. Today it is kept in a glass case for all people to see. You can find this document in Washington, D.C.

Primary Source Review

1 How can you tell that the Constitution is old?

2 Why do you think George Washington signed the Constitution first?

3 How do you know that the first three words are important?

Our Government

Vocabulary

- judge
- President
- Congress
- bill
- court
- Supreme Court
- trial
- jury

Our government is run by three different groups of people. Each group has its own special work to do. The three groups are leaders, lawmakers, and **judges**. Judges decide what the laws mean.

President George Washington

President Abraham Lincoln

Our leaders, lawmakers, and judges work in three different places. They work for our country, our state, and our community. In this lesson you will learn about the leaders, lawmakers, and judges who work for our country.

The leader of our country is the **President**. The President's job is to make sure everyone follows our country's laws. We vote to choose our President once every four years.

 What three groups of people run our government?

President Franklin Roosevelt

President George W. Bush

Making Laws

We also vote for our lawmakers. All of our country's lawmakers together are called **Congress**.

Lawmakers make laws for the people of our country. First they write a **bill**. A bill is an idea for a new law. The lawmakers, or Congress, vote on the bill. If more lawmakers vote "yes" than "no," the bill is given to the President.

Our first Congress

If the President agrees with the bill, the bill becomes a law. If the President does not like the bill, the bill goes back to Congress. Then lawmakers can vote on the bill a second time. If at least two thirds of the lawmakers vote "yes," the bill becomes a new law.

 **What is Congress?**

Congress today

Being Fair

Judges work in a building called a **court**. The most important court in our country is the **Supreme Court** in Washington, D.C. The judges who work here make sure that our laws agree with our constitution.

Judges have **trials** in court. A trial is a meeting to decide if someone broke the law.

Sometimes citizens are chosen to listen to the trial. They are called a **jury**. The jury works with the judge to decide what is fair. If someone broke the law, the judge and jury decide on a punishment.

Supreme Court judges

Our Constitution says that our leaders, lawmakers, and judges must work together. That way one part of our government will not have more power than another.

Lawmakers

**The
Three Parts
of Government**

Leaders

Judges

 What does a jury do?

Lesson Review

① Who is the leader of our country?

Big Idea ② Why do the three parts of our government work together?

③ **Sequence** What happens if the President does not agree with a bill?

Problem Solving

A **problem** is something you need to think about. You **solve** a problem when you find an answer to it. There are three steps to solving a problem.

Step 1 Name the problem.
Ann is the leader of her soccer team. Ann and her team cannot decide what to name their team.

Step 2 List different choices.
• Ann could pick the name because she is the leader.

• Team members could put names in a paper bag. One member could close her eyes and pull out one name.

• The team could vote on a name.

Step 3 Think and solve the problem.
Everyone on the team should have a say, not just Ann. If one name is pulled from the bag, the other players might not like it. So Ann and her friends will vote to choose the team name.

Tigers

Tigers	IIII
Tornadoes	III
Sharks	TTTT I

Try the Skill

1 What is the first step in solving a problem?

2 Why is it a good idea to list different choices?

3 How did Ann and her team solve the problem?

169

2.3.1 Explain how the United States and other countries make laws, carry out laws, determine whether laws have been violated, and punish wrongdoers.

Our Country's Capital

Vocabulary

capital

Capitol

White House

The city of Washington, D.C., is the **capital** of the United States. A capital is the city where the people of our government work. The capital city of Washington, D.C., belongs to all people in the United States.

Supreme Court

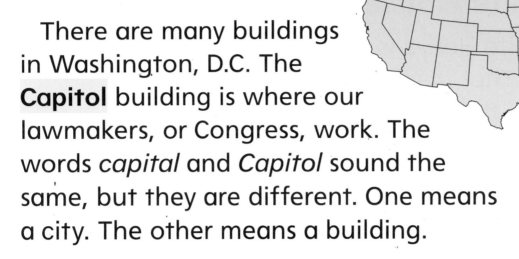

There are many buildings in Washington, D.C. The **Capitol** building is where our lawmakers, or Congress, work. The words *capital* and *Capitol* sound the same, but they are different. One means a city. The other means a building.

The Supreme Court building and the **White House** are also located in Washington, D.C. The President lives and works in the White House.

What three important buildings are in Washington, D.C.?

Capitol building

White House

The White House

The White House is a government building. That means it belongs to all citizens of the United States. Many people visit the White House every year. Here are some of the rooms that visitors can see in the White House.

 Which room do you like best? Why?

The State Dining Room can seat up to 140 people.

The White House Library has many books.

President Lincoln's wife bought this bed. This room is called the Lincoln bedroom.

The President works in the Oval Office.

Lesson Review

1. In what building does Congress work?
2. Why is Washington, D.C., an important city?
3. **Find the Main Idea and Details** What rooms can a visitor find in the White House?

A Child in the White House

Long long ago Tad Lincoln moved into the White House. He was only eight years old. His father was Abraham Lincoln, our sixteenth President. Tad liked to play games at the White House.

When Tad was ten years old, a turkey was brought to the White House. Tad played with the turkey and named it Jack.

When Tad found out that Jack would be eaten, he ran to his father. President Lincoln stopped his work. He wrote an order to save the turkey.

Every year the President of the United States saves one turkey from becoming part of Thanksgiving dinner. This is now a White House tradition.

President Clinton saves a turkey.

Write About It! Why did President Lincoln write an order to save the turkey?

For more about life in the White House, visit:

2.3.1 Explain how the United States and other countries make laws, carry out laws, determine whether laws have been violated, and punish wrongdoers.

Our State Capitals

Vocabulary

governor

You already know that the capital city of Washington, D.C., belongs to everyone in our country. But did you also know that each of our 50 states has its own capital city?

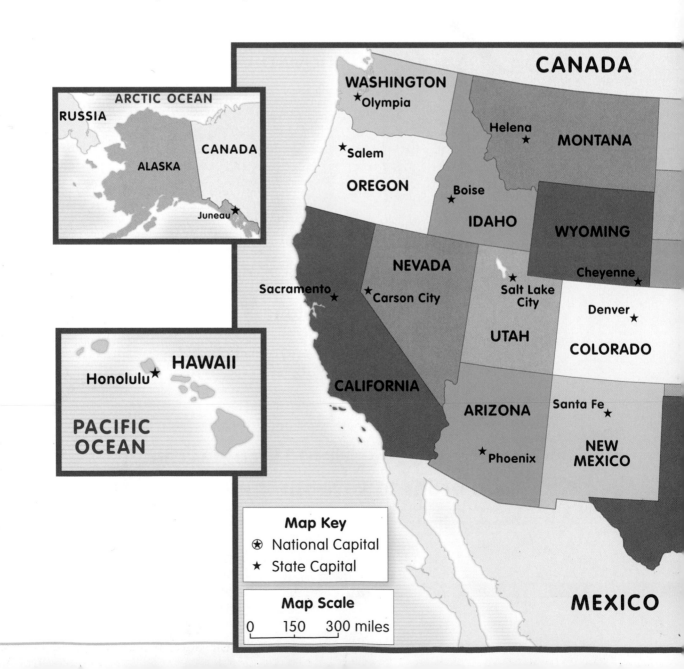

ARCTIC OCEAN

RUSSIA

CANADA

ALASKA

Juneau★

WASHINGTON
★Olympia

Helena ★

MONTANA

★Salem

OREGON

Boise ★

IDAHO

CANADA

WYOMING

Cheyenne ★

NEVADA

Sacramento ★

★Carson City

Salt Lake City ★

Denver ★

UTAH

COLORADO

HAWAII

Honolulu★

PACIFIC OCEAN

CALIFORNIA

ARIZONA

Santa Fe ★

★Phoenix

NEW MEXICO

MEXICO

Map Key
⊛ National Capital
★ State Capital

Map Scale
0   150   300 miles

Every state has its own capital city.
Every capital city has its own capitol
building where the state leaders,
lawmakers, and judges work.

 **What is the capital
of California?**

How is a state
capital shown
on the map?

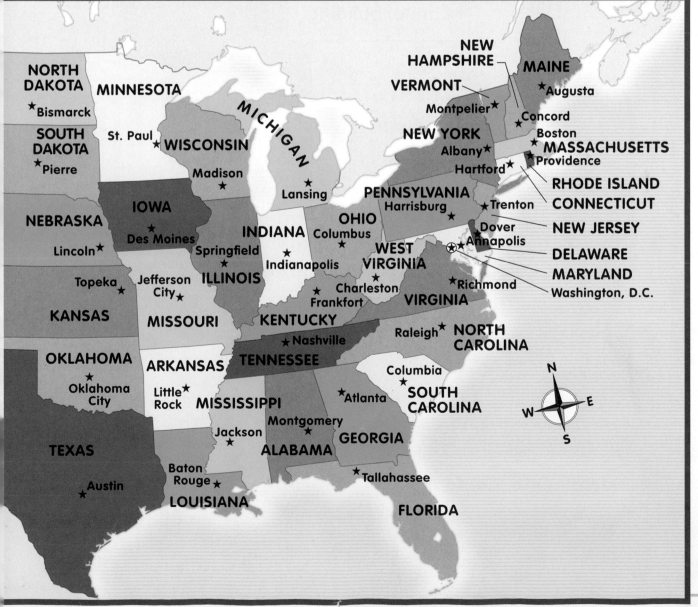

NORTH DAKOTA
★Bismarck

MINNESOTA
St. Paul ★

SOUTH DAKOTA
★Pierre

WISCONSIN
Madison ★

MICHIGAN

NEW HAMPSHIRE

VERMONT
Montpelier ★

MAINE
★Augusta

Concord ★

NEW YORK
Albany ★

Boston
★MASSACHUSETTS
★Providence

Hartford ★

RHODE ISLAND
CONNECTICUT

Lansing ★

NEBRASKA
Lincoln ★

IOWA
★Des Moines

INDIANA
Springfield ★

PENNSYLVANIA
Harrisburg ★

★Trenton
NEW JERSEY

Dover ★
★Annapolis

DELAWARE

OHIO
Columbus ★

Indianapolis ★

WEST VIRGINIA
★Charleston

MARYLAND
Washington, D.C.

Topeka ★
Jefferson City ★

ILLINOIS

Frankfort ★

★Richmond
VIRGINIA

KANSAS

MISSOURI

KENTUCKY

Raleigh ★ NORTH CAROLINA

OKLAHOMA
Oklahoma City ★

ARKANSAS
Little Rock ★

TENNESSEE
★Nashville

Columbia ★

Atlanta ★

SOUTH CAROLINA

N
W E
S

MISSISSIPPI
Jackson ★

Montgomery ★
ALABAMA

GEORGIA

TEXAS

Baton Rouge ★

Austin ★

LOUISIANA

★Tallahassee

FLORIDA

The Capital of California

Sacramento is the capital city of California. The Capitol building in Sacramento is where the state leaders and lawmakers work. It is in a big park. Trees from all over the world grow there. The trees are symbols of the people from all over the world who moved to California.

California's Capitol building

Sacramento, California

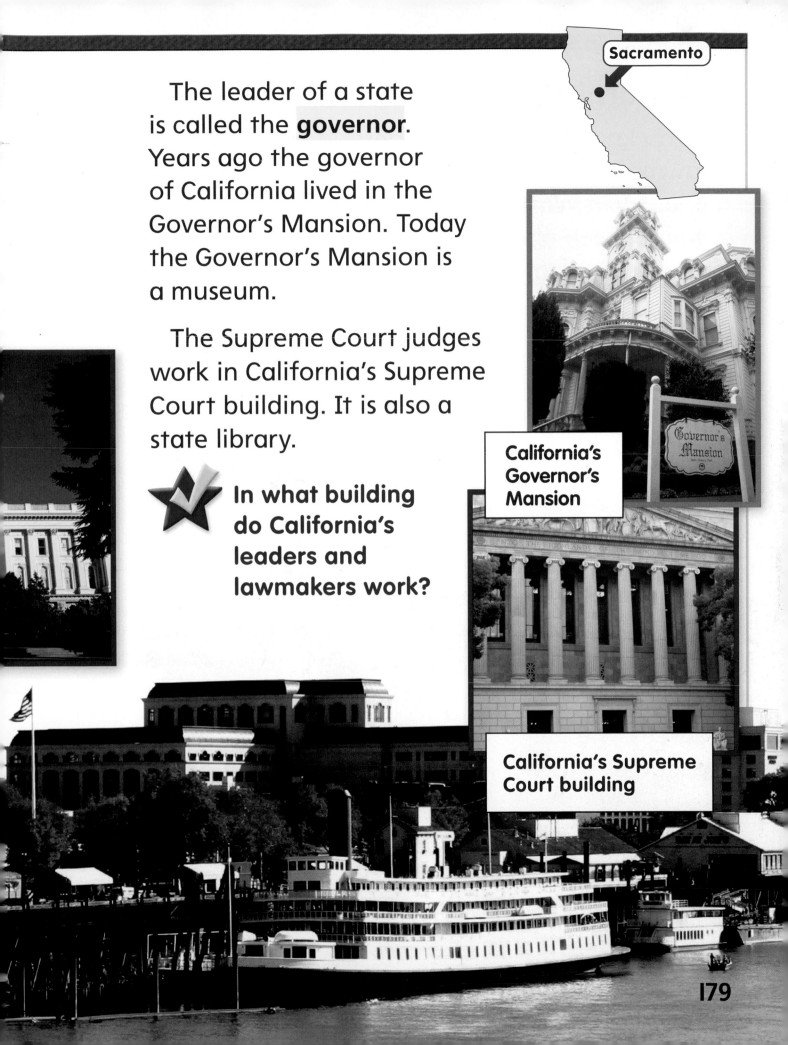

The leader of a state is called the **governor**. Years ago the governor of California lived in the Governor's Mansion. Today the Governor's Mansion is a museum.

The Supreme Court judges work in California's Supreme Court building. It is also a state library.

In what building do California's leaders and lawmakers work?

Sacramento

Governor's Mansion

California's Governor's Mansion

California's Supreme Court building

California State Government

You know about the leaders, lawmakers, and judges who run our country in Washington, D.C. Now you will find out about the three parts of California's state government.

The governor of California is the leader. The governor makes sure that all the people in the state follow the California Constitution and other state laws.

California's lawmakers make ideas for laws, or bills. Then they vote on them. If they vote "yes" on the bills, they give them to the governor. If the governor agrees, the bill becomes a law.

Governor Arnold Schwarzenegger

California's judges have trials to decide if someone has broken California's laws. If someone has broken the law, the judges decide on a fair punishment.

California Lawmakers

California Governor

The Three Parts of California Government

California Judges

What part of the government makes bills?

Lesson Review

1. What happens if the governor agrees with a bill?

2. What are the three parts of California government?

3. **Compare and Contrast** How are the United States government and the California government alike? Different?

Use Diagrams

A **diagram** is a picture with labels. **Labels** tell what things are. A diagram can tell you how something is made or how it works.

The diagram on the next page shows a courtroom. To read the diagram, look at a number. Then find the label that goes with the number in the box below.

Try the Skill

1 Where does the judge sit?

2 Why does the court reporter sit in the middle?

3 **Activity** Make a diagram of your classroom. Label five things.

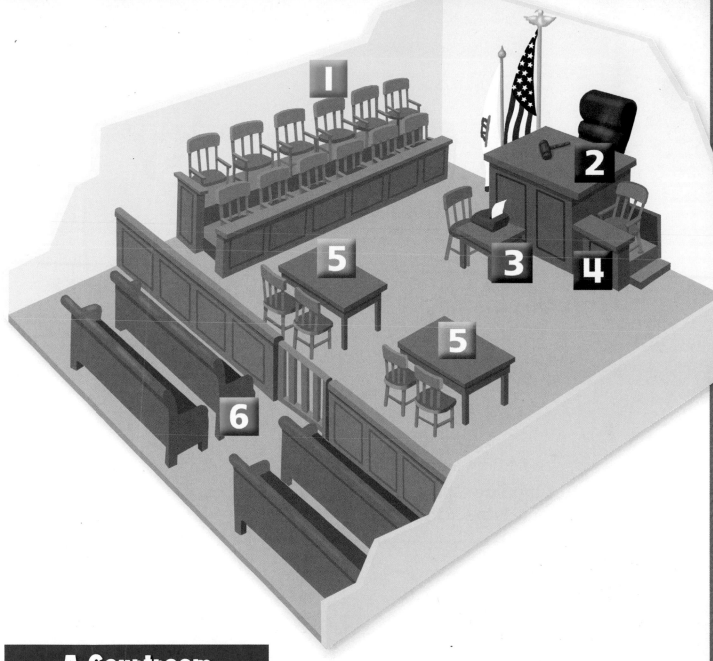

1 Jury Box The jury sits here to listen.

2 Judge's Bench The judge's desk is called a bench.

3 Court Reporter Desk The court reporter records, or writes, everything that is said.

4 Witness Stand A witness is a person who tells what they know. They promise to tell the truth.

5 Legal Tables The people who are on trial and their lawyers sit at these tables.

6 Gallery This area is where people who watch the trial sit.

2.3.1 Explain how the United States and other countries make laws, carry out laws, determine whether laws have been violated, and punish wrongdoers.

A Community Government

You know how our government works for our country and our state. In this lesson you will find out how people in the community of Harlem, New York solved a problem.

Morningside Park in Harlem, New York

Workers in Harlem had taken down bus shelters to fix the street. But the shelters were never put back! People got wet and cold waiting for the bus in the rain and snow. The citizens of Harlem wanted to solve this problem.

 What problem did the citizens of Harlem want to solve?

The Community Board

Some people who live in Harlem belong to a community board. A community board is a group of people who work for the citizens of the community.

Citizens in the community pay money to the government. This money, called **tax**, can be used to help the community. The citizens of Harlem asked the community board to use tax money to fix the bus shelters.

Members of the community board
had a meeting. They told the New York
transportation workers about the problem.
The transportation workers understood
the problem. They agreed to fix the bus
shelters. Tax money was used to get the
job done.

 What is tax money?

An Answer to the Problem

Members of the community board solved the problem. First they had a meeting to talk about the problem. Then they asked the transportation workers to build new bus shelters. Today the citizens of Harlem can stay warm and dry in the cold and rain with the new bus shelters.

Stanley Gleaton is the leader of the community board in Harlem. He says, "Your community board is here to help you with any problems you find. You and your parents can always call if you need help. The community board is here for you!"

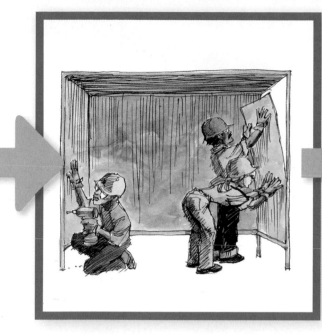

 Do you know who to call to help solve a problem in your community?

Lesson Review

1. What problem did the citizens of Harlem have?

Big Idea 2. What did Harlem's community board do to solve the problem?

3. **Cause and Effect** How do the new bus shelters help the people of Harlem?

Being Honest

Being honest means to tell what is really true even if it is not easy. If you are an honest person, you feel good about yourself.

Mr. Star's class voted to collect food for needy families. Find out what happened when Mr. Star asked Bill and Maria to count the boxes of food.

There are 12 boxes of these yummy raisins. One box would not be missed.

Food for Needy Families

What did Bill and Maria decide to do about the raisins? Were they honest? What do you do with things that do not belong to you?

Citizenship Activity

Make a poster showing a time you saw someone being honest. Label your poster.

Yes, but the raisins do not belong to us.

You are right. These raisins belong to the needy families.

LESSON 6

2.3.1 Explain how the United States and other countries make laws, carry out laws, determine whether laws have been violated, and punish wrongdoers.

Governments of Other Countries

Vocabulary

artifact

The United States and Canada are neighbors. The United States and Canada share a border.

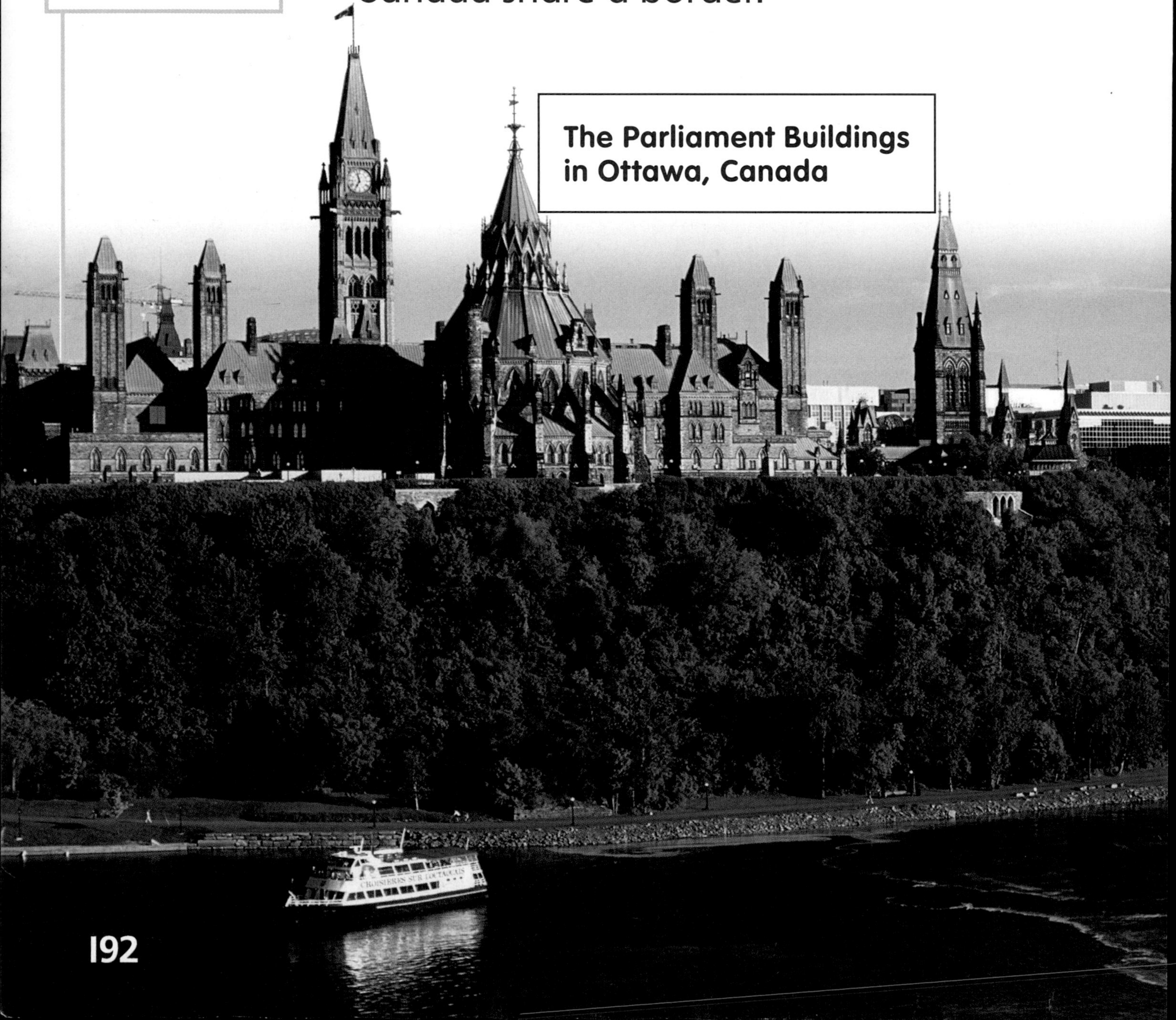

The Parliament Buildings in Ottawa, Canada

Canada has a capital city just like the United States. Ottawa is the capital city of Canada. Canada's leaders, lawmakers, and judges meet in Ottawa.

A long time ago Canada's leaders were kings and queens. Today the people vote for their leaders, just like we do. The leader of Canada is called the Prime Minister. The lawmakers in Canada are called Parliament. Parliament is like Congress in the United States.

What is the leader of Canada called?

Canada

Canada's Parliament

Prime Minister Paul Martin of Canada

Our Neighbor to the South

Mexico is our neighbor to the south. Mexico and the United States share a border.

Mexico City is the capital of Mexico. Mexico's leaders, lawmakers, and judges meet in Mexico City.

Like the United States, the leader of Mexico is called the president. Mexico, however, votes for a new president every six years.

President Vicente Fox of Mexico

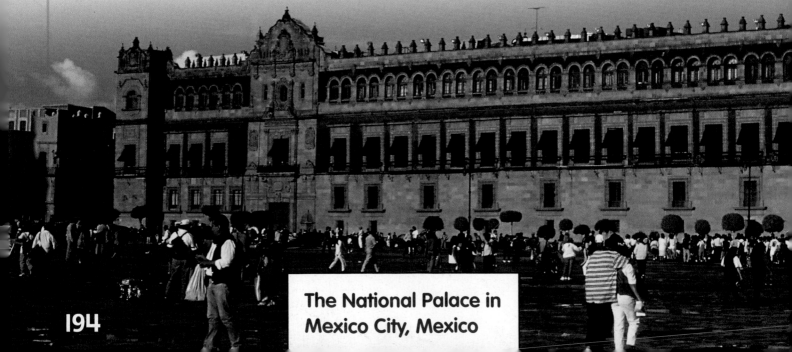

The National Palace in Mexico City, Mexico

Mexico

Mexico's Congress of the Union

The lawmakers in Mexico are called the Congress of the Union. They are like Congress in the United States.

Where do Mexico's leaders, lawmakers, and judges meet?

A Problem in Mexico

Like the United States, the citizens of Mexico work together to solve problems. Not long ago, Mexico had a problem. Visitors in Mexico took important **artifacts** from Mexico's past.

Artifacts are things made by people a long time ago, such as tools and handmade crafts. Visitors to Mexico dug up artifacts from Mexico's land. Some took them home. Others sold them to make money.

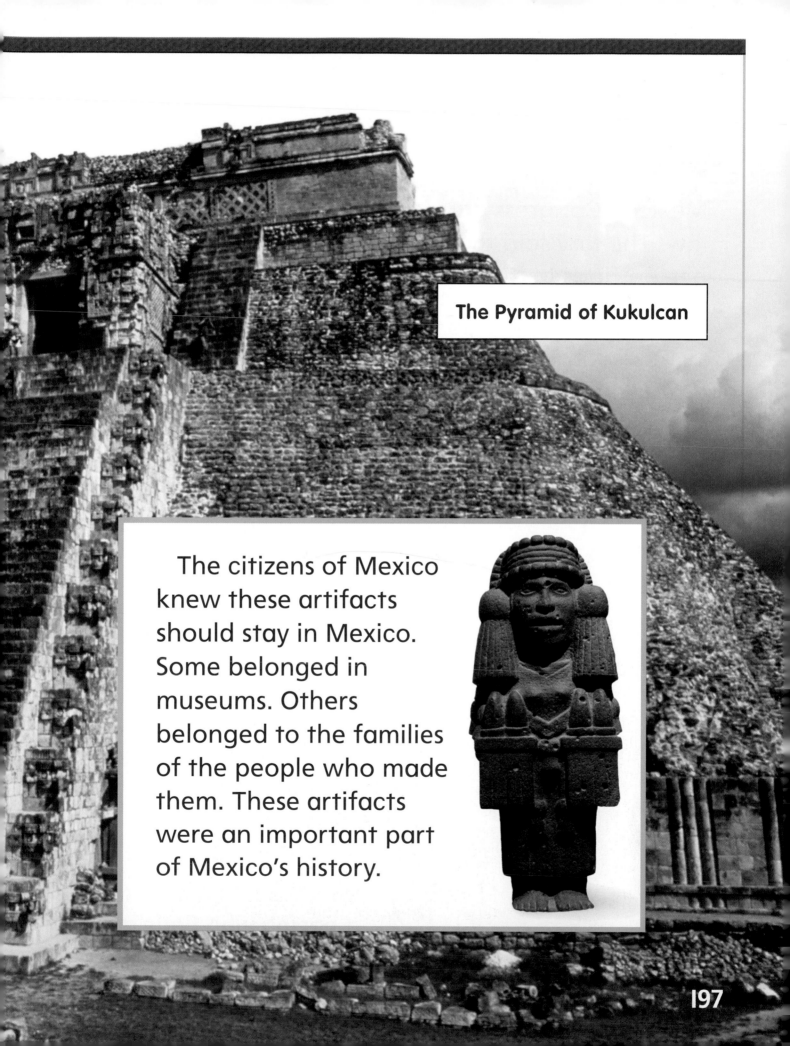

The Pyramid of Kukulcan

The citizens of Mexico knew these artifacts should stay in Mexico. Some belonged in museums. Others belonged to the families of the people who made them. These artifacts were an important part of Mexico's history.

Mexico Solved the Problem

The Mexican lawmakers talked about the problem. In 1972 the lawmakers in the Mexican Congress passed an important law. The law said that any artifact a person finds in Mexico belongs to Mexico.

If someone takes an artifact, it is the same as stealing. The person can be arrested. Arrest means to take a person to jail.

Now Mexican artifacts stay in Mexico. The people of Mexico can study these artifacts in museums. People in Mexico can learn about their past.

Mexican artifact

 What could happen to a person who finds a Mexican artifact and takes it home?

The name of this artifact is "Stone of the Sun."

Lesson Review

1. What country to the south shares a border with the United States?

Big Idea 2. Which part of the Mexican government worked to solve Mexico's problem?

3. **Find the Main Idea and Details** What problem did Mexico solve?

Golda Meir

Golda Meir was a great leader. When she was 70 years old she became the prime minister of Israel. Israel is a country in the continent of Asia.

Golda was Jewish. She was born in Russia. Many Jewish people in Russia were not treated fairly. When she was eight years old her family moved to the United States.

Using Primary Sources

"There is nothing Israel wants so much as peace."
—Golda Meir

Jerusalem is the capital of Israel.

Golda grew up in the United States. She never forgot about how Jewish people were treated in Russia. When she was an adult she decided to help Jewish people from all over the world.

Golda had meetings with other Jewish people about having a home country. Together they made a plan to go back to Israel, a land where Jewish people had once lived long ago.

 Why did Golda Meir want to help Jewish people?

Golda Meir was the prime minister of Israel from 1969 to 1974.

LOG ON

For more about Golda Meir, visit:

www.macmillanmh.com/ss/ca/bios

2.3.2 Describe the ways in which groups and nations interact with one another to try to resolve problems in such areas as trade, cultural contacts, treaties, diplomacy, and military force.

Working Together

People need to **cooperate**. Cooperate means to work together. Sometimes people do not agree with each other. They can respect each other's ideas and cooperate to work things out.

For example, there was a community that had an empty lot. Some people in the community wanted to make it into a playground for children. Others wanted to turn it into a dog park so that dogs could run freely.

The two groups met to talk about the problem. They decided to cooperate. The group who wanted the playground agreed to build smaller slides. This way some room would be left for the dogs to run.

The people who wanted the dog park agreed that the dogs could run in a smaller area. Now the community has both a playground and a dog park!

 What problem did the two community groups have?

Countries Work Together

People in different countries need to cooperate too. For example, polar bears only live in Canada, Denmark, Norway, the United States, and Russia. Too many polar bears were being hunted and killed each year.

In 1965 people from the five countries had a meeting. They talked about the problem. They made a list of things they could do to save the polar bears.

In 1973 all five countries signed a law that would protect the polar bears. These five countries cooperated. They talked about the problem and did not fight. Today they still work together to keep the polar bears safe.

 In what five countries do polar bears live?

Lesson Review

1. Why did the polar bears need protection?

2. How did the community cooperate about the empty lot problem?

3. **Sequence** What three things did the people from the five countries do in 1965? Tell what happened first, next, and last.

The Chunnel

Characters

Pierre, leader from France • **Anne,** leader from England • **Sandra,** English inspector • **Leon,** French inspector • **Michelle,** French worker • **James,** English worker

Narrator: It is 1988. There is a meeting between leaders from England and France. They have a problem to solve.

Pierre: (pounds his fist on the table) Our countries are so close. Why does the trip take so long? We must make the trip shorter.

Anne: Yes, but how? Have you forgotten? There is water between our countries. The English Channel of course!

(French and English inspectors, Sandra and Robert, burst into the room. They are holding drawings of a tunnel.)

Sandra: What if we made a tunnel?

Leon: Yes! A *tunnel* can go under the *channel*.

Anne: Tunnel?

Pierre: Channel?

Anne and Pierre together: Let's call it a chunnel! Bring in the workers.

(French and English workers, Michelle and James, come into the room.)

Pierre: Michelle, you begin digging from France.

Machine used to dig the Chunnel

Anne: James, you dig from England. You will meet each other in the middle.

Michelle: It could be many years before we see each other again, James. Adieu, my friend.

James: Good luck Michelle, old chum. Race you to the middle!

(The English and French teams start digging very hard.)

Narrator: It was a long time before they met in the middle. It was three years, to be exact. The English got there first.

James: Wow! This is the middle. I wonder where my friend Michelle is?

Narrator: Suddenly the French worker, Michelle, breaks through.

Michelle: (shaking dust off of herself)
Is that you, my English friend?

James: Yes. It is so good to see you. It has been a long time.

Michelle: We did it! We have connected our countries!

Leon: This is the longest tunnel in the world. And the safest!

Sandra: Best of all, we made it together! We could not have done this alone.

(The inspectors shake hands. The workers come and shake hands with each other.)

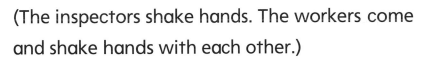

Narrator: In 1994 the Chunnel opened. It was a huge success. The English and French had wanted to make a tunnel for hundreds of years. By working together they were able to get it done.

Write About It!

Write a story about a tunnel from your neighborhood to anywhere in the world that you would like to go.

A Government in Europe

Some countries in Europe decided to work closely together. The countries formed a group called the European Union. These countries keep their own laws. But together they also follow special European Union laws. The map on the next page shows the flags of the 25 countries that are in the European Union.

Most of the countries in the European Union use the same kind of money, called the *Euro*. This makes it easier for people to travel and do things in each other's country.

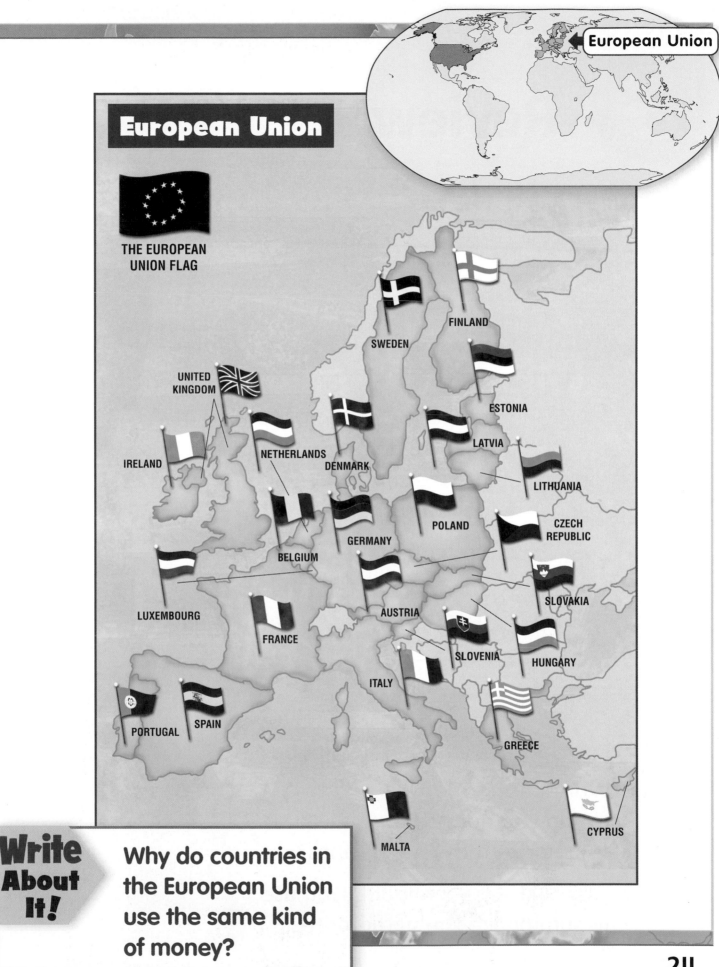

European Union

THE EUROPEAN UNION FLAG

SWEDEN

FINLAND

UNITED KINGDOM

ESTONIA

IRELAND

NETHERLANDS

DENMARK

LATVIA

LITHUANIA

POLAND

CZECH REPUBLIC

GERMANY

BELGIUM

LUXEMBOURG

SLOVAKIA

FRANCE

AUSTRIA

SLOVENIA

HUNGARY

ITALY

PORTUGAL

SPAIN

GREECE

MALTA

CYPRUS

Write About It!

Why do countries in the European Union use the same kind of money?

Reading Social Studies

Summarize

Read the paragraphs. Then answer the questions.

Mr. Good asked the children working in the Art Center to clean up. Sean helped Tanya clean off the tables. Lisa and Donna washed the paint brushes.

The children working in the Art Center cooperated. They worked together.

Art Center
Keep Me Clean!

1 What information would you not use to summarize these paragraphs?

2 What information would you use to summarize the paragraphs?

Choose the word that best tells about each sentence.

trial   governor   cooperate

3 The leader of a state is called the _____.

4 A _____ is a meeting to listen to a problem and decide if someone broke the law.

5 _____ means to work together.

Critical Thinking

6 How is the President of the United States chosen?

7 Suppose a community wanted to open a public library. Where could they get the money to pay for it?

8 Write sentences telling how the United States government and the California government are alike. Write about how they are different.

2.3.1

Chart and Graph Skills **Use Diagrams**

Look at the diagram on the next page. Then answer the questions.

1 A White House guest might have dinner in which room?

A   Blue Room

B   State Dining Room

C   Green Room

D   Red Room

2 What did President Monroe do in the Green Room?

A   ate dinner

B   had meetings

C   played cards

D   got married

3 Which is the largest room in the White House?

A   East Room

B   Red Room

C   Green Room

D   State Dining Room

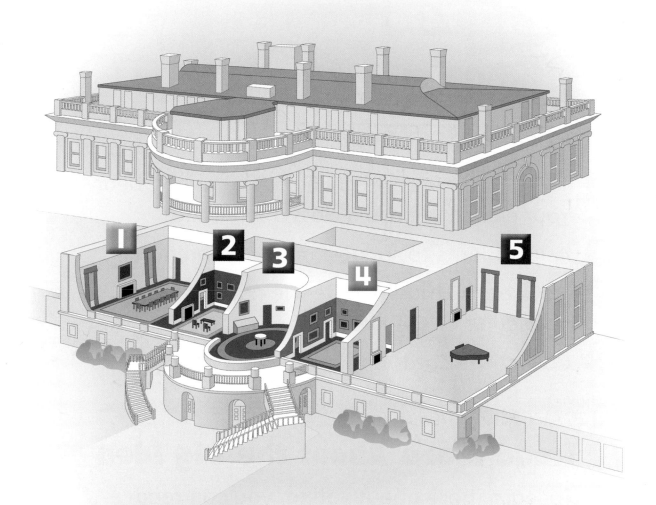

The White House

1. **State Dining Room** The President and guests eat dinner here.
2. **Red Room** The President's wife meets her guests in the red room.
3. **Blue Room** President Grover Cleveland had his wedding in this room.
4. **Green Room** President James Monroe liked to play cards in the green room.
5. **East Room** The East Room is the largest room in the White House.

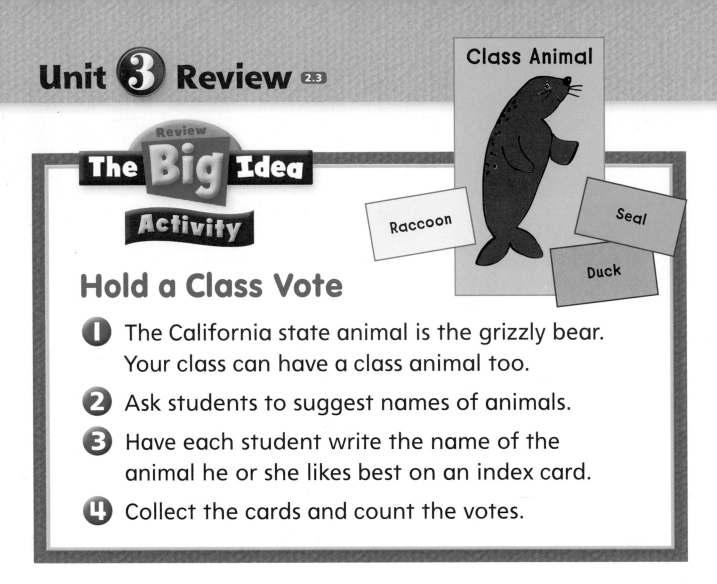

Class Animal

Raccoon

Seal

Duck

The Review **Big** Idea Activity

Hold a Class Vote

1. The California state animal is the grizzly bear. Your class can have a class animal too.

2. Ask students to suggest names of animals.

3. Have each student write the name of the animal he or she likes best on an index card.

4. Collect the cards and count the votes.

Read More About the Big Idea

To learn more about voting, you can read one of these books.

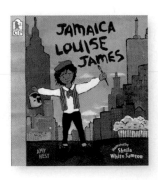

LAUNCH PAD For help with the Big Idea activity visit:

www.macmillanmh.com/ss/ca/launchpad

UNIT
4

2.4 Students understand basic economic concepts and their individual roles in the economy and demonstrate basic economic reasoning skills.

Our Needs and Wants

Explore
The Big Idea

How do we get the things we need and want?

People supply what we need and want.

How do we get the things we need and want?

Vocabulary

needs

wants

Needs are things that people must have to live. **Wants** are things people would like to have, but do not need. Read about some ways we get the things we need and want.

"I put my money away so I can use it later."

218

"We pay the builder to build us a new home."

"Mom and I shop at stores to buy the things we need and want."

Every person has needs and wants.
In this unit you will find out how we get
the things we need and want.

Literature

The Adventures of Johnny Appleseed

by Karen Lowther

illustrated by Erika LeBarre

Long ago there lived a man named John Chapman. John loved plants, animals, and the outdoors.

When John was a young man, many people were just starting to move West. John wanted to help these people.

He got an idea. He decided to plant apple seeds so they could have apples.

Soon John Chapman had a nickname. People began to call him Johnny Appleseed.

Many people say Johnny Appleseed wore a tin pot on his head and no shoes. Others say he wore clothes made from old coffee sacks and never trimmed his beard.

Johnny bought apple seeds from cider mills in Pennsylvania. Cider mills are places where apples are crushed to make apple cider. The mills do not use the apple seeds.

He packed up his seeds and paddled along the Ohio River. He knew that the soil close to the river would help grow very healthy trees.

Johnny roamed through parts of Ohio, Indiana, and Illinois. Johnny looked for perfect places to plant his apple seeds.

When Johnny found a place he liked, he camped there for many weeks. He chopped weeds. He dug up soil and planted rows and rows of apple seeds.

Johnny always came back to the places where he planted seeds. He was happy to find tender young apple trees. Each year he trimmed their branches until they began to flower. When the petals fell, apples grew in their place. Soon ripe apples dotted the states of Ohio, Indiana, and Illinois.

Some say Johnny gave away apple trees for free to people who had no money. Others say he traded apple trees for clothing or other things he needed.

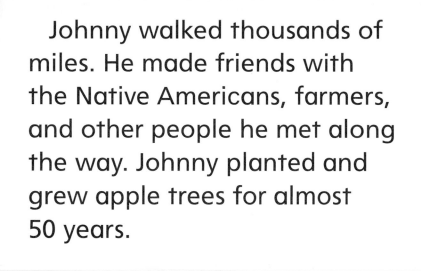

Johnny walked thousands of miles. He made friends with the Native Americans, farmers, and other people he met along the way. Johnny planted and grew apple trees for almost 50 years.

Talk About It! How did Johnny Appleseed use apple seeds to help people?

Vocabulary
About Economics

Read the words in the boxes. Then find the pictures in the big photographs.

A **producer** makes or grows things to sell. (page 272)

A **crop** is a group of plants grown for food. (page 239)

A **product** is something made or grown.
(page 262)

A **factory** is a building where things are made.
(page 273)

Write About It!

What do you see in these pictures?

Sequence

The **sequence** tells the order in which things happen. The sequence tells what happens first, next, and last.

To tell the sequence,

- Read the paragraph.

- Find what happened at the beginning.

- Find what things happened in the middle.

- Find what happened at the end.

Put the information in a chart like the one shown below.

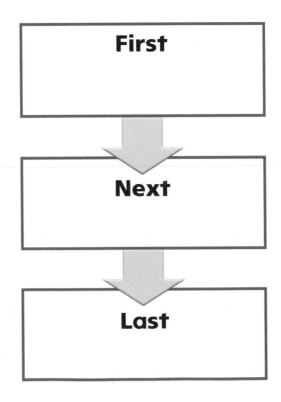

First

Next

Last

Read the paragraph below. Then try the skill.

A farmer planted tomato seeds. Soon the seeds grew into tall plants. One day green tomatoes grew on the plants. When the tomatoes turned red, the farmer picked them.

Try the Skill

1. What happened first?
2. What happened after the seeds grew into tall plants?
3. Why is it helpful to find the sequence?

2.4 Students understand basic economic concepts and their individual roles in the economy and demonstrate basic economic reasoning skills.

Making Choices

This family has food, clothing, love, and **shelter**. Shelter is a place where people live. These are needs that all people have.

Vocabulary

shelter

choice

scarce

save

goods

services

People have wants too. We can not always have everything we want.

Sometimes people need to make a **choice**. A choice means to pick something from a number of things. The boy below is making a choice between two kinds of fruit he wants.

Why do people need to make choices?

Saving for Choices

Ana wants a CD player. But she does not have enough money to buy one. When there is not enough of something, it is called **scarce**. Ana's money is scarce.

There is something you can do when money is scarce. You can **save** your money. Save means to keep your money to use later.

Ana does not have enough money.

Ana got a job raking leaves for neighbors after school. She is paid money for her work.

Ana made a plan to save her money. Each time she earns money, she will put some of it away. Soon she will have enough money to buy the CD player.

 What can you do when money is scarce?

Ana saves her money.

Ana buys the CD player!

233

Goods and Services

The things we buy are called **goods**. Goods can be made or grown. Food, clothing, books, and toys are all goods. People use money to buy goods.

People also use money to buy **services**. A service is something useful that people do for others. There are many different kinds of service work.

Every community has doctors, barbers, taxi drivers, teachers, firefighters and police officers. They are all service workers. Each of them does something useful for others. They are paid money for the services they do.

 What is service work?

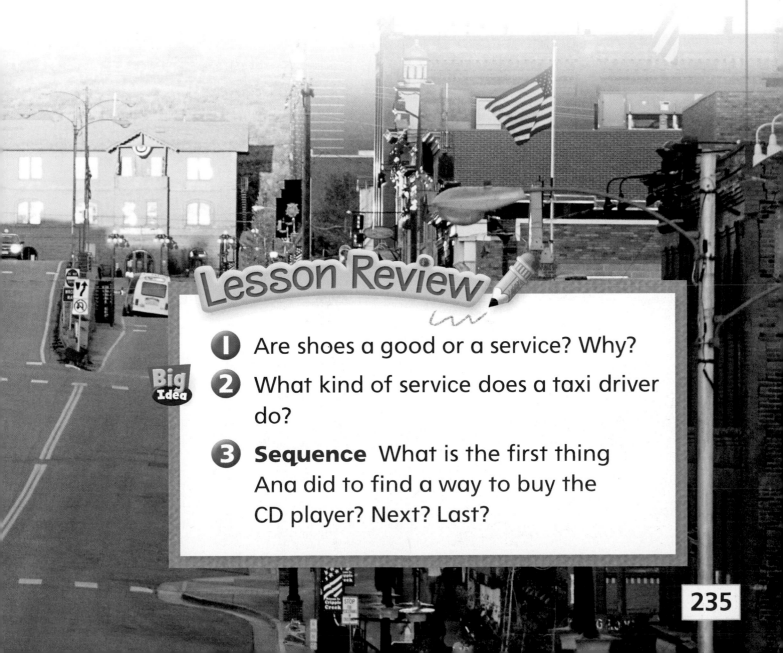

Lesson Review

1. Are shoes a good or a service? Why?

2. What kind of service does a taxi driver do?

3. **Sequence** What is the first thing Ana did to find a way to buy the CD player? Next? Last?

Use the Dictionary

A dictionary tells the meaning of words. It also tells how to spell words and how to use words in sentences.

Learn the Skill

1 Look at the dictionary page. Each word starts with the letter **s**. Then the words are in ABC order by the second letter, the third letter, and so on.

2 The two words at the top of the page are called *guide words*. They tell you the first and last words on the page.

3 Two sentences follow each word. The first sentence tells you what the word means. The second sentence is an example sentence. It shows how the word can be used.

save You save when you keep something to use later. I will **save** my money to buy a pair of skates.

scarce When there is not enough of something, we say it is **scarce**. Water was **scarce** in the desert.

service A service is something useful that people do for others. One **service** a doctor does is to help people when they are sick.

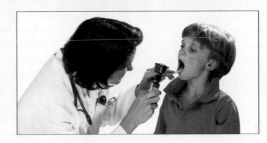

shelter A place where people live is called a shelter. Our house is a **shelter**.

Try the Skill

1. What are the guide words?
2. What does **scarce** mean?
3. In what order are words listed in a dictionary?

Farming Yesterday and Today

People from long, long ago had to work very hard to meet their needs. They hunted, fished, and picked plants every day to feed their families.

One group of people lived in a place called Mesopotamia. They were the very first people to make bread.

They found grain that was good to eat. Grain is seed found in some plants, like wheat and rye. They found a way to use the grain to make bread.

This tool was used to cut down plants with grain.

238

This art shows Mesopotamians tending crops.

First they crushed the grain. This made flour. Then they added water to make bread. Finally they cooked the bread over a fire.

Farmers planted some of the grain to grow new **crops**. Crops are plants that are grown for food. When there was no rain, farmers had to bring water from nearby rivers to water the plants.

 What did the farmers do when it did not rain?

239

Planting and Harvesting

The people of Mesopotamia used stones to crush grain into flour. It took hours to do this by hand. Many years later mills were invented. Mills are machines that crush things. A person had to work hard turning a wheel on the mill to crush the grain. Later people found out how to use water to turn the mill's wheel.

Stone for crushing grain

Mill with water wheel

Technology has made big changes in farming. Technology is using science to make things faster, easier, or better. Technology has helped farmers. Machines can plant seeds. Machines can cut and pick up plants with grain. Today machines do much of the work that people used to do by hand.

 How did the people of Mesopotamia crush grain?

Machine for planting seeds

Machine for cutting plants

The grain is stored in a silo.

Grain to Flour

After the grain is removed from the plant, it is stored in a tall building called a silo.

It is much faster to crush the grain into flour today. Machines made of steel crush the grain. Then the crushed grain is shaken. Out falls the flour!

Steel machines crush the grain.

Flour is poured into bags.

This baked bread was made with flour.

The flour is refrigerated to keep it cold and fresh. Then the flour is put into bags. It is sent to bakeries, grocery stores, and restaurants.

 Why is flour refrigerated?

Lesson Review

1 What is technology?

Big Idea **2** How is flour made from grain today?

3 Sequence Name three steps people in Mesopotamia followed to make bread.

Use Flow Charts

A **flow chart** is a kind of chart. A flow chart shows the order in which things happen, or flow.

This flow chart shows how bread is made. To read the chart, look at number l. It shows flour being mixed with yeast and water or milk to make bread dough. What is the next step?

❶ Flour, yeast, and water or milk are mixed to make bread dough.

❷ The dough is shaped into loaves.

1 What happens after the dough gets larger?

2 What is the second step in the flow chart?

3 **Activity** Make your own flow chart of something you know how to make.

3 The loaves are placed in a warm area to rise. Rise means to get larger.

4 The bread is baked in the oven.

George Washington Carver

George Washington Carver was born on a farm in Missouri. George learned to love all growing things on the farm. People asked him to come to their houses to help their sick plants. They called George "The Plant Doctor."

When George tried to go to college, he was turned away because of the color of his skin. George had great courage. He went on to find another college. There he studied hard and became a great scientist. He discovered over 300 ways to use peanuts, including how to make peanut butter.

Carver taught college students about farming. He invented a way to keep farm soil healthy. Because of his invention, farmers today can grow more and healthier crops.

 How did George Washington Carver help farmers?

LOG ON For more about George Washington Carver, visit:

www.macmillanmh.com/ss/ca/bios

Using Primary Sources " My very soul thirsted for an education. . . . I wanted to know every strange stone, flower, insect, bird, or beast. " —George Washington Carver

2.4.1 Describe food production and consumption long ago and today, including the roles of farmers, processors, distributors, weather, and land and water resources.

From Farm to Home

Vocabulary

orchard

Apples are grown on farms called **orchards**. You learned that apple trees can grow from seeds when you read "The Adventures of Johnny Appleseed." But it takes a long time for apple trees to grow from seeds.

① The farmer attaches branches to the new apple trees.

Farmers found a faster way to grow apples. They cut branches from a grown tree. Then they attach the branches to a young tree. This is called *grafting*. Soon flowers appear on these branches. The flowers turn into apples.

 What is grafting?

 **Chart and Graph Skills**

What happens after the tree gets flowers?

2 Flowers grow on the branches.

3 The flowers turn into apples.

Picking and Moving the Apples

When the apples are ready to pick they are so heavy that the tree branches almost touch the ground. The apple picker climbs up a ladder and picks each apple by hand. The apples are put into a sack worn by the picker.

Pickers empty their bags of apples into boxes. When the boxes are full, they are put on a truck.

4 Apple pickers put the apples into sacks.

5 Apples are loaded into boxes.

The truck driver brings the apples to a big refrigerator where they are kept cold. Then the apples are washed and put into crates. Finally a truck carries the crates of apples to a store.

 How are the apples kept cold?

 What happens before the apples are loaded into boxes?

6 Boxes of apples are driven to a big refrigerator.

7 Apples are delivered to grocery stores.

Making Apple Pie!

Apples are put out in stores for people to buy. There are many kinds of apples. Each kind is grouped together.

8 Apples are put out for sale in stores.

9 A family buys the apples to make a pie.

This family bought apples from the store. They cut the peel off the apples. Then they cut the apples into slices. They put the apple slices in a pie crust and baked the pie in the oven.

After dinner everyone had a piece of apple pie!

Chart and Graph Skills

What is the last step in the flow chart?

10 The apple pie is baked and ready to eat.

How do you make an apple pie?

Lesson Review

1 What is an orchard?

Big Idea **2** Why do farmers use grafting instead of growing apple trees from seeds?

3 **Sequence** What does an apple picker do first? Next? Last?

Follow Routes on a Map

A **route** is a way of going from one place to another. You can follow a route on a map. Orange arrows show the route on this map.

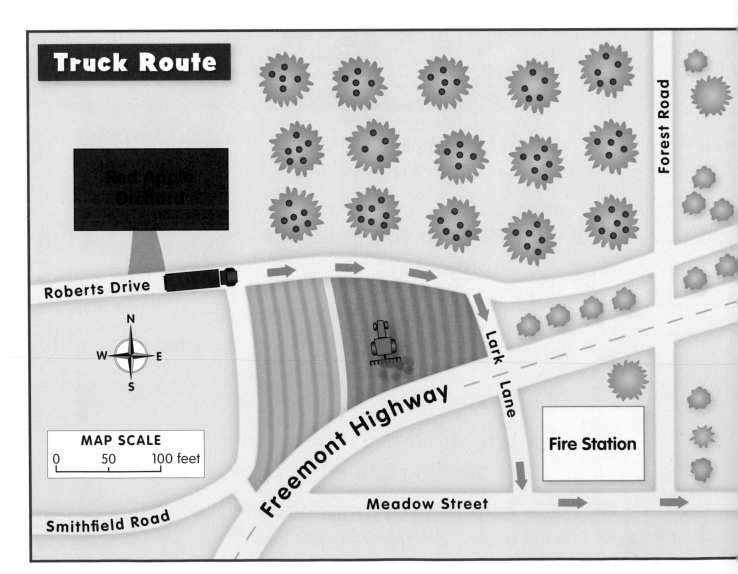

Truck Route

Red Apple Orchard

Forest Road

Roberts Drive

N W E S

Lark Lane

Freemont Highway

Fire Station

MAP SCALE
0   50   100 feet

Meadow Street

Smithfield Road

Find the Red Apple Farm truck on Roberts Drive. Now find the Farmers' Market on the map. The driver is bringing apples to the Farmers' Market to sell. Follow the arrows from the Red Apple Farm truck to the Farmers' Market.

⋯ Try the Skill ⋯⋯⋯⋯⋯⋯⋯⋯⋯⋯⋯⋯⋯⋯

1 What highway will the driver pass while driving on Lark Lane?

2 On what street is the Farmers' Market?

3 **Activity** Make your own map. Show a route a truck might follow from your house to a store.

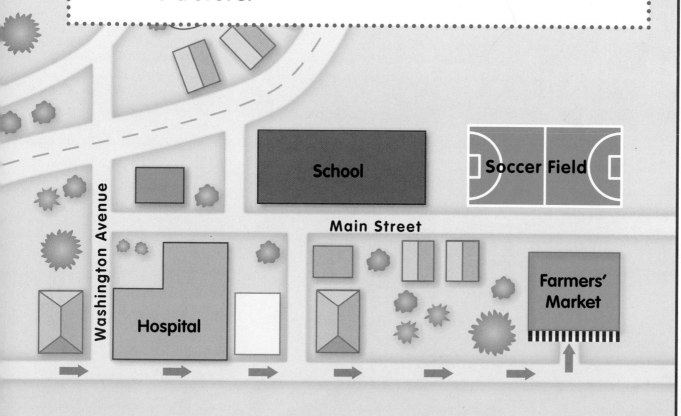

255

2.4.1 Describe food production and consumption long ago and today, including the roles of farmers, processors, distributors, weather, and land and water resources.

Dairy Farming

Vocabulary

dairy farm

pasteurize

A **dairy farm** is a special farm for dairy cows. Dairy cows make milk.

It takes a lot of work to run a dairy farm. Farmers feed the cows with grain and hay. They also let the cows eat fresh grass in a field.

Feeding the cows

Dairy farm

256

Twice a day the cows are milked. Cows can be milked by hand, but most farmers use milking machines. This keeps the milk clean. The machines put the milk into tanks. The milk can stay cold in the tanks.

What is one job of a dairy farmer?

Milking machines

Preparing the Milk

There are special trucks that keep milk cold. They take the milk from the farm to a building where the milk is put into large tanks.

Long ago a man named Louis Pasteur found out that heat kills germs. Because of this, the milk in the tanks gets **pasteurized**, or heated, to kill any germs.

Milk being pasteurized in tanks

After the milk is quickly heated, it is poured into bottles or cartons. The milk needs to be made cold again. Next the bottles are taken to stores to sell.

Why is the milk heated?

Milk being poured into bottles

Other Uses for Milk

Milk can be used to make other things. You can add things to milk that make the milk change into solid pieces. These pieces are called cheese. Milk can also be used to make things such as yogurt, cottage cheese, and ice cream.

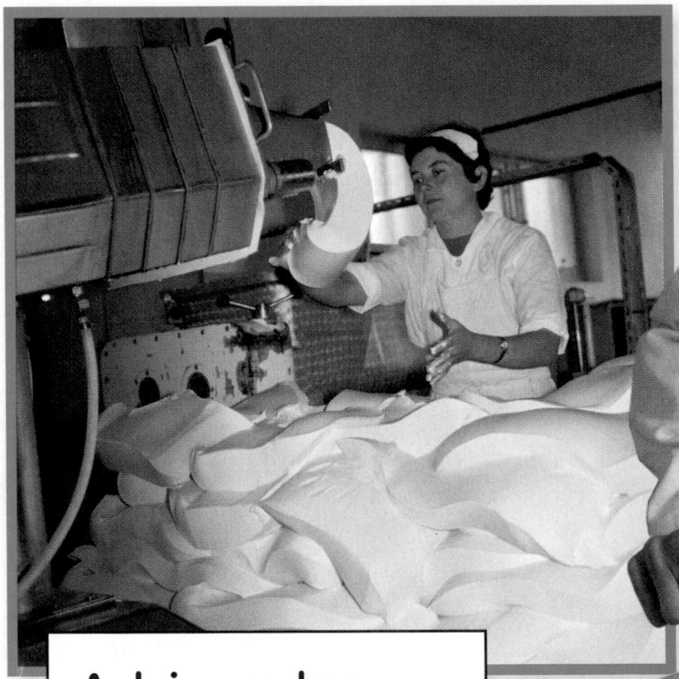

A dairy worker takes fresh butter from the machine.

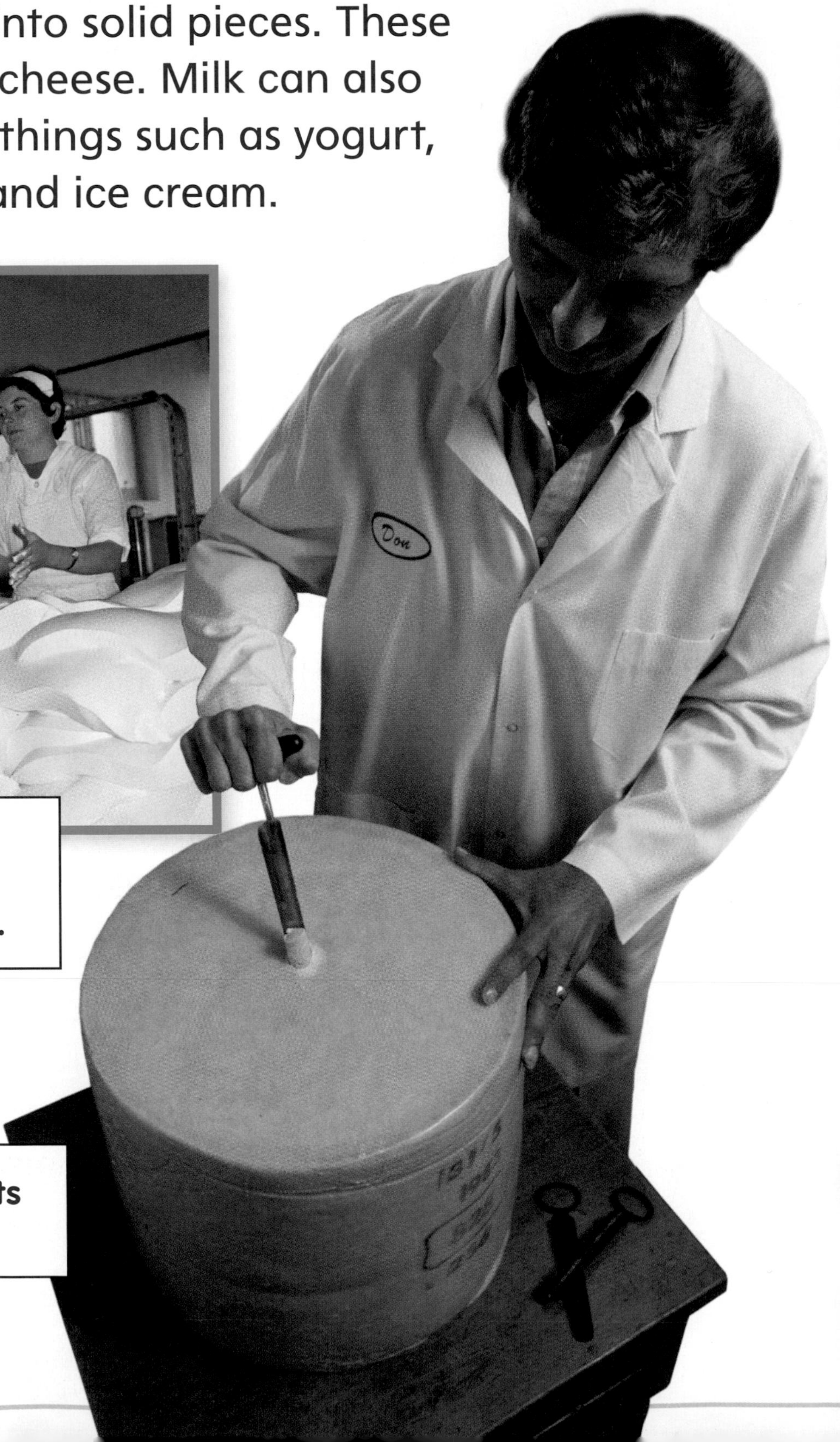

A cheesemaker tests the cheese.

If you let milk stand for a while, cream will rise to the top. Cream can be used by itself, or it can be mixed or whipped to make whipped cream. If you whip the cream long enough, it turns into butter!

 Name a food that is made from milk.

Lesson Review

1 What did Louis Pasteur find out?

Big Idea

2 Where does a glass of milk come from?

3 **Cause and Effect** What effect does heat have on milk?

Use Product Maps

A **product** is a good, or a thing, that is made or grown. The map on the next page shows products that are grown in California. The products on this map are fruits and vegetables. Product maps have symbols that stand for different products.

The map key shows the kinds of products you can find on this map. Find the citrus fruit symbol on the map key. Fruits like oranges, lemons, and grapefruit are called citrus fruit. Now find citrus fruit symbols on the map.

Try the Skill

1 Citrus fruit grows between which two cities?

2 In what part of California do potatoes grow?

3 Do you think you might see more cows near San Diego or Fresno?

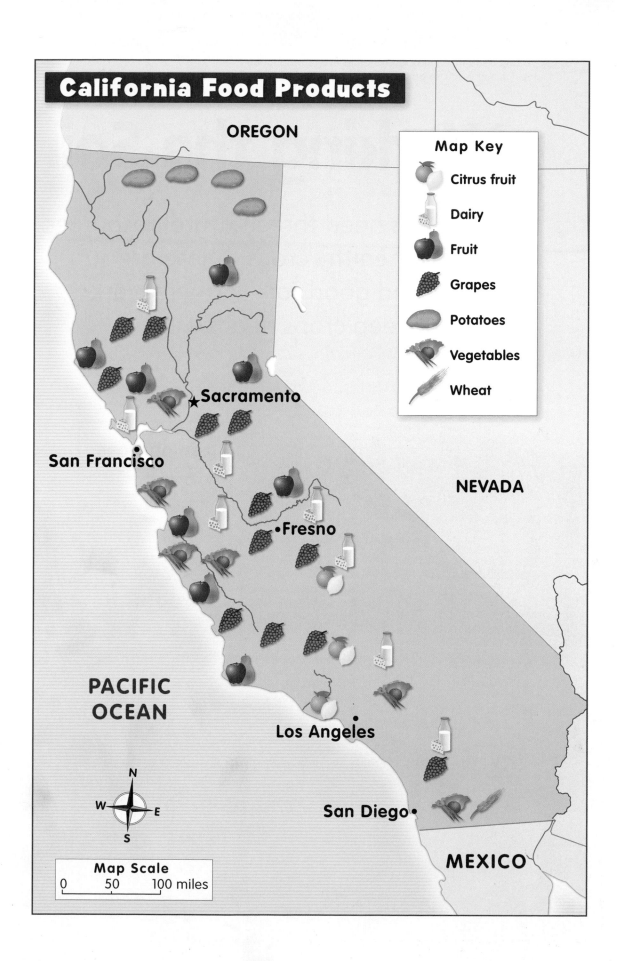

California Food Products

OREGON

NEVADA

PACIFIC
OCEAN

MEXICO

★ Sacramento

San Francisco

•Fresno

Los Angeles

San Diego•

Map Key
- Citrus fruit
- Dairy
- Fruit
- Grapes
- Potatoes
- Vegetables
- Wheat

N
W E
S

Map Scale
0   50   100 miles

5

Working the Soil

Vocabulary

irrigation

strike

Farmers need three natural resources to grow healthy crops. These are sun, water, and good soil. Farmers work hard to keep crops healthy.

Lemon trees

Fruits like oranges, grapefruit, lemons, and grapes grow best in warm weather. These four fruits are grown in California orchards. The sun keeps them warm and healthy.

Sometimes the weather turns cold. Farmers make small fires in pots called smudge pots. They place the pots by the trees. This keeps the fruit from freezing.

 When would a farmer use a smudge pot?

Smudge pots

Crops Need Water and Food

Some areas have good soil, but not enough rain for the crops to grow. The farmers in these areas use special machines to put water into the soil. This is called **irrigation**.

Farmers must know when and how much to water the crops. Too much irrigation, rain, or floods can also kill crops.

Irrigating the soil

Adding plant food to the soil

Some areas have enough water, but the soil is not good. Farmers make the soil better by mixing it with special plant food.

 What can a farmer do if the soil is not good?

A Farm Emergency

Farmers face many problems. They can have bad storms, fires, and strikes.

To **strike** means to stop working. Sometimes workers go on strike when they feel they are not treated fairly. This is their right. But if fruit pickers go on strike, no one picks the fruit. Then the fruit goes bad.

Fruit pickers on strike

Sometimes there are bad storms or fires. If this happens where fruit trees grow, the fruit can die.

Farmers can lose money because of storms, fires, and strikes. The fruit is scarce. The price for products, like grape jam and orange juice, goes up. People who buy from the farmers lose money too. They have to pay high prices for the products.

 How can a storm affect the price of food?

Lesson Review

1. What would a farmer do if the soil was good, but there was no rain?

Big Idea 2. What do farmers need to grow healthy crops?

3. **Make Predictions** A farmer grows lemon trees. The lemon pickers go on strike. What might happen to the lemons?

Celebrate Farmworkers
2.4.1 with a Poem

This poem is about farmworkers. Farmworkers work long and hard picking fruits and vegetables for us to eat.

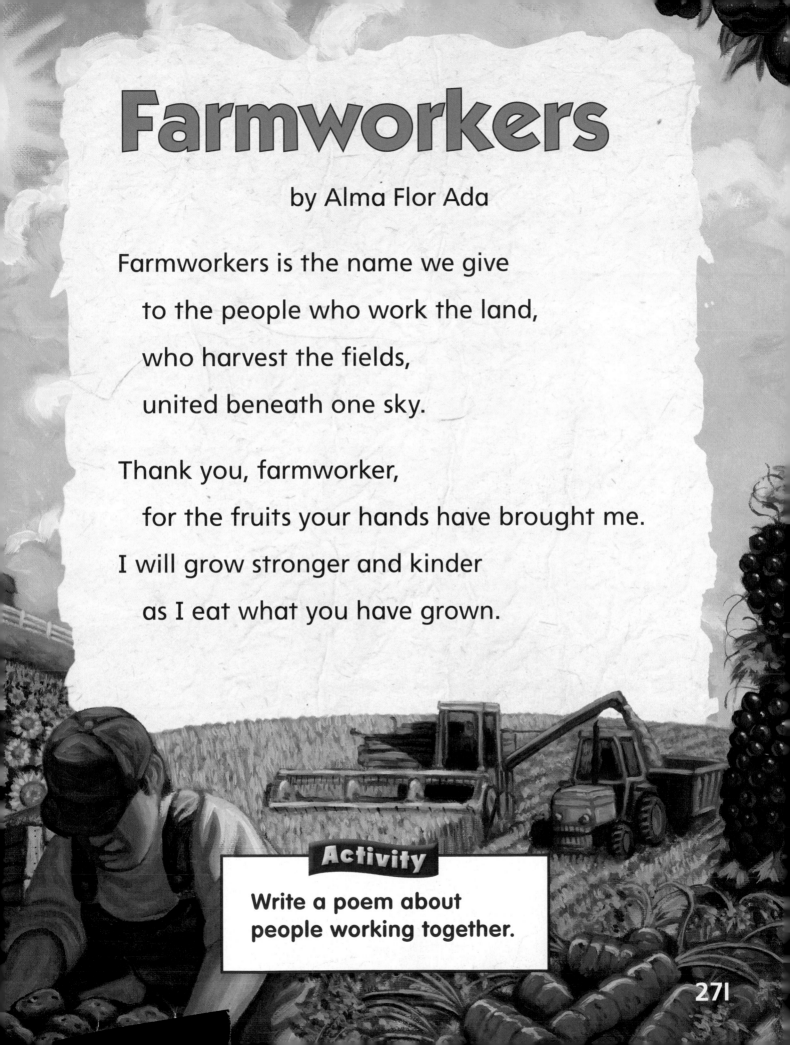

Farmworkers

by Alma Flor Ada

Farmworkers is the name we give

to the people who work the land,

who harvest the fields,

united beneath one sky.

Thank you, farmworker,

for the fruits your hands have brought me.

I will grow stronger and kinder

as I eat what you have grown.

Activity

Write a poem about
people working together.

LESSON

6

2.4.2 Understand the role and interdependence of buyers (consumers) and sellers (producers) of goods and services.

Producers and Consumers

A **producer** makes or grows products, or goods, to sell. This farmer is a producer. She grows grapes to sell.

Grape farm

272

Some of her grapes are sent to a **factory**. A factory is a building where things are made.

At the factory, workers make the grapes into grape jam. Then they put the grape jam into bottles. The workers are also producers. They are making grape jam to sell.

 Why is a farmer called a producer?

Factory worker

Getting Ready for Market

This potter is also a producer. He makes pottery to sell.

The farmer and potter can sell their products or goods to a store or market. Then people will come to the store or market to buy the goods.

Pottery

A **consumer** uses the products, or goods, made by a producer. Consumers eat or use things that are grown or made by producers.

 How do you know the girl is a consumer?

We Are All Consumers

Everyone is a consumer. That is because we all have needs and wants.

When the farmer grows grapes to sell, she is a producer. But when the farmer buys a piece of pottery that she wants, she is a consumer.

When the potter makes things for people to buy, he is a producer. But when the potter buys and eats the grapes, he is a consumer.

 Why are we all consumers?

Lesson Review

1. Name one thing made by a producer that you have bought.

Big Idea 2. What would happen if we did not have enough producers?

3. **Compare and Contrast** How are a producer and a consumer different? Alike?

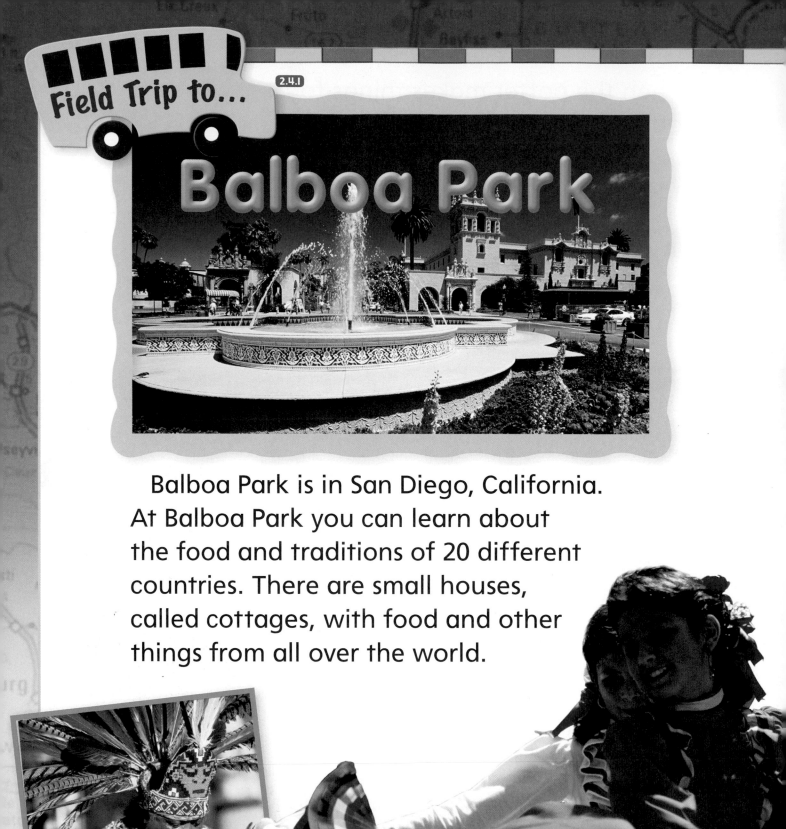

Balboa Park

Balboa Park is in San Diego, California. At Balboa Park you can learn about the food and traditions of 20 different countries. There are small houses, called cottages, with food and other things from all over the world.

San Diego,
California

① Let us look at the beautiful art
in the House of Norway. Are
you hungry? Try some pasta
from the House of Italy!

② Can you hear the
African drummers?
It is hard to sit still.
The music makes you
move your feet.

279

3 You can go to a Japanese tea ceremony. Do not forget to take off your shoes! You can sit on a special mat on the floor. A cup of tea is poured from a beautiful pot. Everyone gets a small cup of tea to drink. Bow "thank you" as you walk out the door.

4 Look around you. You might find something from Mexico or China. What a great place to learn about other cultures!

What kinds of jobs might a worker at Balboa Park do?

Balboa Park

LOG ON For more about Balboa Park, visit:

www.macmillanmh.com/ss/ca/fieldtrips

2.4 Students understand basic economic concepts and their individual roles in the economy and demonstrate basic economic reasoning skills.

Trading with Other Countries

In the United States we have lots of factories and farmland. We make and grow many products.

We make and grow more goods than we need. We can **trade** these extra goods with other countries. Trade means to give something and then get something back. When countries trade, they buy and sell goods and services.

Goods from another country

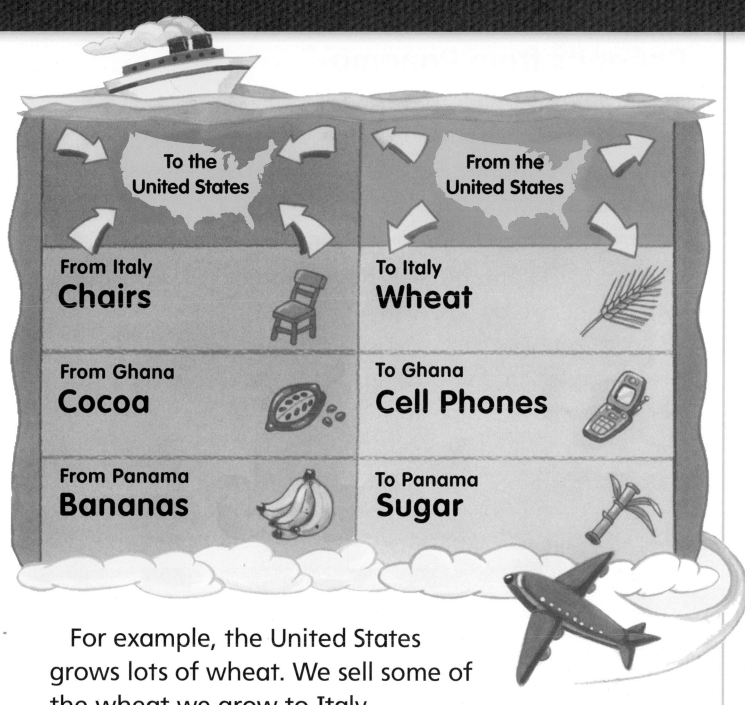

To the United States		From the United States	
From Italy Chairs		**To Italy** Wheat	
From Ghana Cocoa		**To Ghana** Cell Phones	
From Panama Bananas		**To Panama** Sugar	

For example, the United States grows lots of wheat. We sell some of the wheat we grow to Italy. Italy sells chairs to the United States. We trade with Italy.

 What goods does the United States make and grow?

Bananas from Panama

Bananas grow where it is very hot and rainy. It is very hot and rainy in the country of Panama. Farmers there grow bananas. Panama sells bananas to the United States.

Farmers in Panama pick the bananas when they are green. Boxes of bananas are sent on boats to the United States. The bananas arrive in about two weeks. Then they are sent to stores. When they turn yellow they are ready to eat.

Green bananas on a tree

Cutting bananas

The United States sells sugar to Panama. Panama sells bananas to the United States. We trade with Panama.

Panama

How do bananas get from Panama to the United States?

Putting bananas on the boat

Cocoa from Ghana

Ghana is one of the biggest producers of cocoa beans in the world. Cocoa beans can be made into cocoa, candy, and other chocolate products. Ghana sells cocoa beans to the United States.

Cocoa beans are grown on trees. The beans grow inside small cases, called pods, on the trees. Families work together on farms. They cut cocoa pods from the trees. Then they cut open the pods and take out the beans.

Cocoa pods

The United States trades with Ghana. The United States pays money to Ghana for cocoa beans.

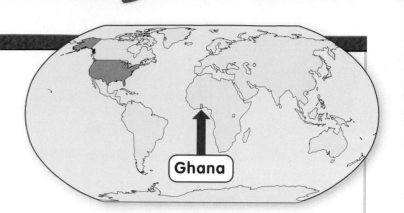

Ghana

 What products are made from cocoa beans?

Chocolate candy made from cocoa beans

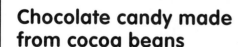 Lesson Review

1. What goods does Panama sell to the United States?

Big Idea 2. Why do we trade with other countries?

3. **Make Predictions** What might happen if there were no workers to pick the bananas?

287

Cooperation

You just learned how countries cooperate by trading. You now know how working together makes things better for everyone. Find out what happened when Juan had to finish his chores.

Can you go with me to play ball?

No, I have to finish raking these leaves.

We can cooperate. You rake and I will bag. Then, we can play ball!

288

How are the boys cooperating? What might happen if the boys do not work together? What good thing will happen because the boys cooperated?

Citizenship Activity

With a partner, imagine that one of you is a producer and one of you is a consumer. Act out how the two of you cooperate so that you are both happy.

FILL TO THIS LINE
TO CLOSE BAG, ROLL DOWN AND CRIMP

FOR LEAVES, GRASS CLIPPINGS, YARD TRASH

BIODEGRADABLE
COMPATIBLE FOR COMPOSTING PROGRAMS
(NO GLASS, METAL, STONES OR PLASTIC)

A Market in Chile

Chile has many places to buy and sell goods. People in Chile can go to a mall, a store, or an outdoor market.

This is an outdoor market in Santiago, Chile. Producers come here from all over Chile to sell goods like crafts, jewelry, and food.

Producers in Chile

Santiago, Chile

Consumers go to the outdoor market to buy the goods that the producers have made or grown. They can buy special things they can not find in stores.

At this market consumers can watch people make baskets, pottery, and other crafts. They can eat a delicious meat pie, called *empanada,* right out of the oven!

Chile

Consumers in Chile

Write About It!

What kind of goods do the producers in Chile bring to the market?

Sequence

Read the paragraph. Then answer the questions.

Pam wanted to help with the school bake sale. She and her mom bought eggs, flour, and raisins at the store. Then they made muffins. When the muffins came out of the oven, Pam put them in boxes. The next day Pam sold all the muffins at the bake sale!

1 What happened first?

2 What happened after the muffins came out of the oven? What happened last?

Vocabulary

Choose the word that best completes each sentence.

goods   scarce   consumer

3 A _____ is someone who uses the goods made by a producer.

4 _____ are things that people make or grow.

5 When there is not enough of something, it is _____.

Critical Thinking

6 How are needs and wants different?

7 Name some kinds of service workers.

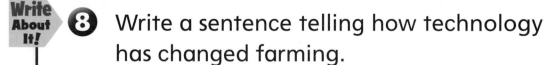

8 Write a sentence telling how technology has changed farming.

2.4.1

Use Flow Charts

Look at the flow chart below. Then answer the questions.

❶ Buying oranges

❷ Oranges are cut in half.

❸ Making orange juice

1 What happened just before the orange juice was made?

    A The orange juice was drunk.

    B The oranges were bought.

    C The oranges were picked from a tree.

    D The oranges were cut in half.

2 What happened just after the orange juice was made?

    A The oranges were bought.

    B The orange juice was drunk.

    C The oranges were picked from a tree.

    D The oranges were cut in half.

3 What was the first thing that happened?

    A The oranges were cut in half.

    B The orange juice was drunk.

    C The orange juice was made.

    D The oranges were bought.

4 **Drinking fresh orange juice**

Goods	Services
I am a baker. I bake bread.	I am a teacher. I teach children.

The Big Idea Activity

A Cartoon

1. Write "Goods" and "Services" on a sheet of paper.

2. Cut out pictures of working people from magazines.

3. Glue a picture of a producer on the "Goods" side, and a service worker on the "Services" side.

4. Write a speech bubble for each worker.

Read More About the Big Idea

To learn more about how we get things we need and want, you can read one of these books.

LAUNCH PAD For help with the Big Idea activity, visit:

www.macmillanmh.com/ss/ca/launchpad

UNIT

5

2.5 Students understand the importance of individual action and character and explain how heroes from long ago and the recent past have made a difference in others' lives.

Many Special People

The Explore Big Idea

How can one person make our world a better place?

Special people who make our world better

297

Explore The Big Idea

How can one person make our world a better place?

Many people do things to make our world a better place. Read about what these children do.

"I spend time helping others."

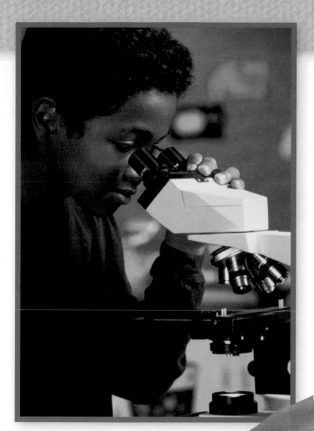

"I study science. One day I will help make sick people better."

"I learn to dance. I can put beauty into the world with my dancing."

In this unit you will find out how just one person can make a difference. You will learn ways that you can make our world a better place to live.

Hold Fast

by Louise Driscoll
illustrated by Liz Conrad

Within your heart

Keep one still, secret spot

Where dreams may go,

And sheltered so,

May thrive and grow—

Where doubt and fear are not.

Oh, keep a place apart

Within your heart,

For little dreams to go.

Your Dreams

Talk About It!

What dreams do you have?

Vocabulary
About Citizenship

Read the words in the boxes. Then find the pictures in the big photographs.

A **volunteer** is a person who works for no pay to help others.
(page 316)

A **scientist** is
a person who
works in a special
part of science.
(page 320)

A **discovery** is
something that
is seen or found
for the first time.
(page 320)

Write About It!

What do you see
in these pictures?

Cause and Effect

A person, thing, or event that makes something happen is called a **cause**. The thing that actually happens because of the cause is called the **effect**.

For example, a baseball player hits a ball over the fence. The baseball player made something happen. The baseball player is the cause. The ball going over the fence is the effect.

To find cause and effect,

- Read the paragraph.

- Find something that happened. That is the effect.

- Decide who or what made the thing happen. That is the cause.

You can put your information in a chart like the one shown below.

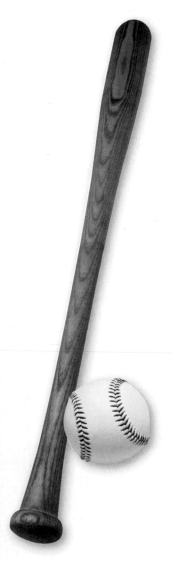

Cause	Effect

Read the paragraph. Then try the skill.

Rachel Carson was a scientist and author. She worried about a poison that was used to kill insects. She knew the poison could hurt other living things. She wrote a book called *Silent Spring*. Her book helped make the world better.

··· Try the Skill ·····

1. What caused Rachel Carson to write the book *Silent Spring*?

2. What effect did her book *Silent Spring* have?

3. Why do you think it is helpful to understand cause and effect?

2.5 Students understand the importance of individual action and character and explain how heroes from long ago and the recent past have made a difference in others' lives.

People Making Differences

Did you know that long ago people walked or rode horses to get around? It took days to get from one place to another! Then a man named Nicholaus Otto made an engine. Later another man, Henry Ford, made a car that could run with Otto's engine.

Henry Ford

Nicholaus Otto

306

Soon after a woman named Mary Anderson found it hard to see out of the car window when it rained. She made windshield wipers.

Mary Anderson

We are so lucky that **individuals** like Otto, Ford, and Anderson made these things. An individual is one person. These individuals have made our lives better.

How did Otto's engine help Henry Ford?

More People Make a Difference

Long ago black and white children did not go to school together. The schools for black children were not as good as schools for white children. Booker T. Washington worked very hard to make good schools for black children.

Booker T. Washington

Laszlo Biro

Does your teacher write with a pen? Years ago people wrote with feathers. The quill of the feather was dipped into ink. It was very messy! Later a man named Laszlo Biro made the first ball point pen.

Long ago William Holmes McGuffey wrote a reading book for children. His books helped children read for about 50 years. Today we can choose from many different reading books.

Our lives would not be easy without these people and many others we may not know. Just one individual can make a big difference in our world!

 Why is a ball point pen easier to use than a feather quill?

William H. McGuffey

① What individual made a car?

Big Idea ② How did William Holmes McGuffey make our world a better place?

③ **Cause and Effect** What caused Mary Anderson to make windshield wipers?

Classify

Classify means to put things that are alike into groups. On this page you see pictures of things in a classroom.

Do you see the *McGuffey Reader?* Now look at the other pictures that are like the Reader. Do you see the dictionary and the textbook? You could name this group "School Books."

Look at the other pictures. They are all items used for the chalkboard. You could name that group "Chalkboard Items."

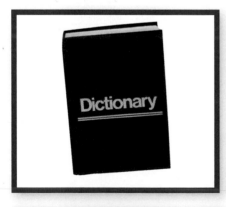

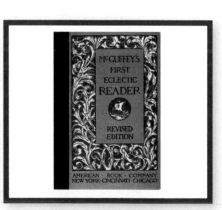

···· Try the Skill ················

Here are six more pictures for you to classify.

1 Find the picture of the ball point pen. Now find two other pictures that are like the pen. What could you name that group?

2 How are the other three pictures alike?

3 What could you name that group?

2

2.5 Students understand the importance of individual action and character and explain how heroes from long ago and the recent past have made a difference in others' lives.

Everyday Heroes

Vocabulary

courage

hero

volunteer

Many people work to make our world a better place to live. Firefighters, police officers, and people in the military do brave things every day to keep us safe. They must have **courage** to do their jobs. Courage is doing something even when you are afraid.

Firefighters

312

Firefighters go into burning buildings. They put out fires and save people. Police officers help people who are in trouble. Military men and women protect our country and our freedom.

Police officer

Military man

These everyday **heroes** make our lives better. A hero is a person who does something brave or important that helps others.

 How does a firefighter show courage?

313

Teachers and Hospital Workers

Teachers work every day to help children. They teach them to read and write. They help children learn about the world.

Teacher

Doctors, nurses, and other hospital workers take care of people who are hurt or sick. They save lives and help people get well.

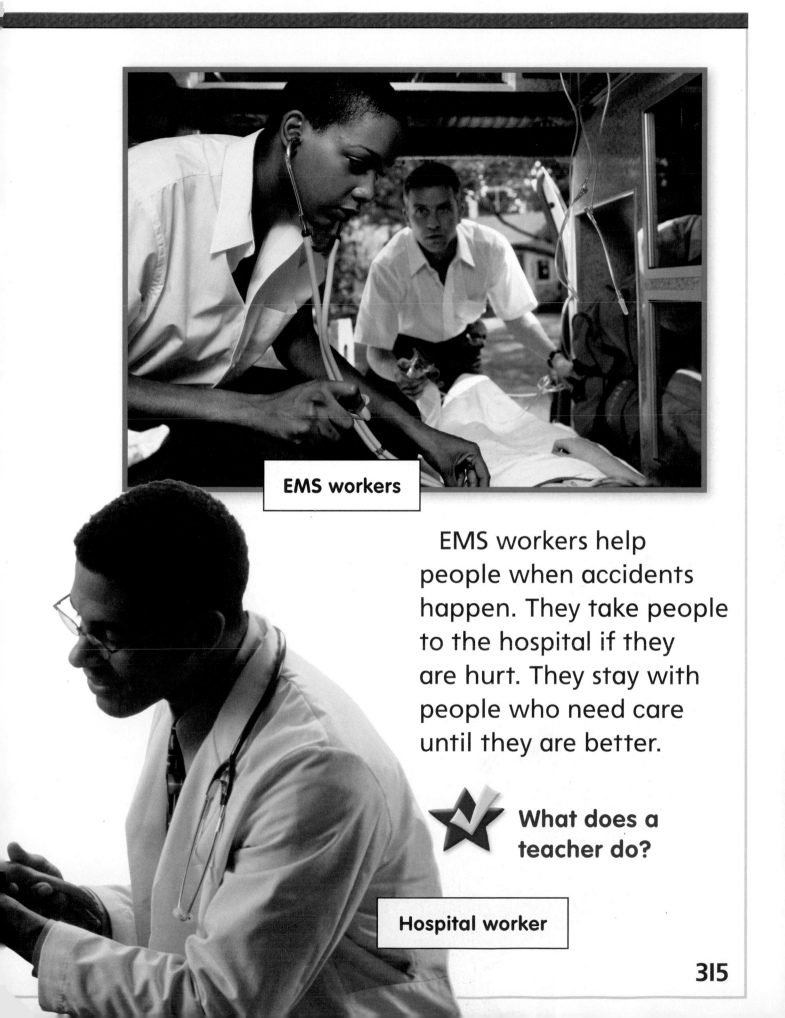

EMS workers

EMS workers help people when accidents happen. They take people to the hospital if they are hurt. They stay with people who need care until they are better.

What does a teacher do?

Hospital worker

315

Volunteers

Volunteers are people who work for no pay to help others. Volunteers spend time helping because they care.

Some volunteers visit older people who are alone. Others help children to read or just play a game!

Children can help too. They can give away their old toys or clothes to children who do not have many. They can clean up the neighborhood or become safety guards at school.

People can help people. Together we can make our world a better place.

 **How can children help?**

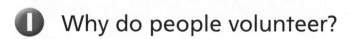

1. Why do people volunteer?

2. What is an everyday hero?

3. **Find the Main Idea and Details**
Find the main idea and details in this lesson.

Helping Police Dogs

Alyssa Mayorga lives in Garden Grove. She found out that a police dog got hurt while helping a police officer. "Police dogs help protect us," she said. "I want to help protect them." She found out that the dogs can wear special vests to help protect them.

Alyssa decided to use her collection of pennies to buy some vests for the dogs. But the vests cost a lot of money.

PENNIES FOR THE
PROTECTION OF POLICE DOGS

All donations will go towards the purchase of bulletproof vests for various police departments whose K-9 officers are not currently vested. We will first vest any K-9 that is already working on the streets, otherwise, we will vest a K-9 out of Adlerhorst Police K-9 Academy of Riverside, CA.

Thank you for your donation.

Making a difference, one penny at a time.

So Alyssa asked other people to help the dogs too. She pasted signs on empty cans and put them in animal hospitals all over town. In less than a year, Alyssa collected enough money to buy ten vests.

Garden Grove, California

Alyssa gave the vests to police officers who worked with dogs. She said, "It feels good to help others."

Alyssa Mayorga

Being a Good Citizen

How do children in your community help others?

Activity

Find out about a problem in your community. Make a plan for how you and your classmates can help.

LESSON

3

2.5 Students understand the importance of individual action and character and explain how heroes from long ago and the recent past have made a difference in others' lives.

Giants of Science

Vocabulary

scientist

discovery

inventor

A **scientist** is a person who works in a special part of science. Important **discoveries** have been made by scientists. A discovery is something that is seen or found for the first time.

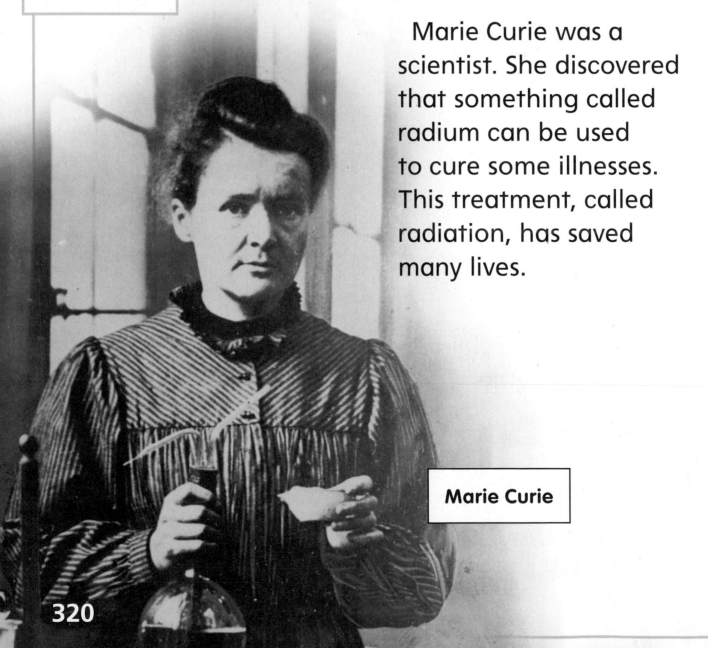

Marie Curie was a scientist. She discovered that something called radium can be used to cure some illnesses. This treatment, called radiation, has saved many lives.

Marie Curie

Albert Einstein was a scientist who was very good at math. Einstein's math helped inventors find ways of using large amounts of electricity all at once.

Charles Drew was a great doctor. He discovered a way to store, or keep, blood. Stored blood has saved lives all over the world.

How did Albert Einstein's math help inventors?

Albert Einstein

Dr. Charles Drew

Inventors

An **inventor** is a person who makes something for the very first time. Thomas Edison and Lewis Latimer were inventors. They discovered how to make a light bulb that could shine for a very long time. There are many other great inventors too.

Thomas Edison

Lewis Latimer

Years ago computers were too large to use in homes. Then Steve Jobs and Steve Wozniak invented the first personal computer. It was small enough to use at home. Today people use computers in homes, schools, work, at coffee shops—almost everywhere!

David Filo and Jerry Yang are friends. Together they made a long list of their favorite Web sites. They decided to put their list into one large Web site. Today many people use this Web site to find new information.

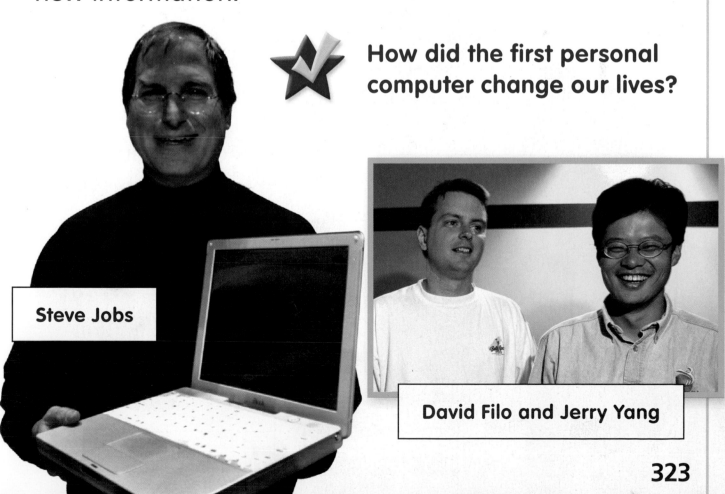

How did the first personal computer change our lives?

Steve Jobs

David Filo and Jerry Yang

Explorers of the Air and Sea

In 1983 Sally Ride became the first American woman astronaut in space. Today she helps young girls learn more about science.

Sally Ride

Jacques Cousteau loved the ocean and all the things living in it. He made movies under water. He helped people learn and care about the ocean.

Jacques Cousteau

Orville and Wilbur Wright

Two brothers named Orville and Wilbur Wright made bikes. They thought riding a bike felt like flying! They used what they knew to make an airplane. Today people fly everywhere in airplanes.

 What special thing did the Wright Brothers do?

Lesson Review

Big Idea

1. How do scientists help people?

2. How did Charles Drew make our world a better place?

3. **Compare and Contrast** How are Sally Ride and Jacques Cousteau alike? Different?

Use the Internet

You can find information on the **Internet**. The Internet is a network of information from all over the world. You need to use a computer to find information on the Internet.

A group of information that is found together in just one place on the Internet is called a **Web site**. Each Web site has its own address, called a **URL**. The URL is made up of letters, numbers, and symbols. You can use the keyboard of your computer to type in the URL. Then you click on the "Go" arrow. You will now see the Web site. You can use **browser buttons** to go back and forth between two Web sites.

To use the Internet,

- Click on the address bar.
- Type in a Web address or URL.
- Click on the "Go" arrow.

Click on the "Back" browser button to go back to the first Web site. Click on the "Forward" browser button to go to the next Web site.

Browser buttons

Web site address or URL

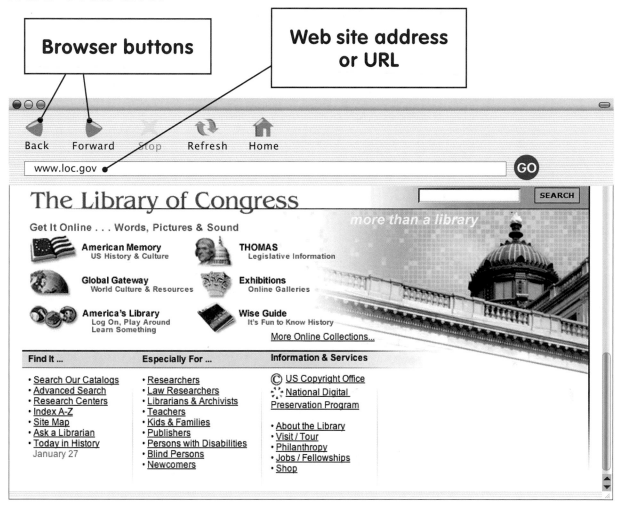

Try the Skill

1 What is the URL for this Web site?

2 What can you learn about on this Web site?

3 Why might you want to use a browser button?

Dr. Fleming Saves the Day

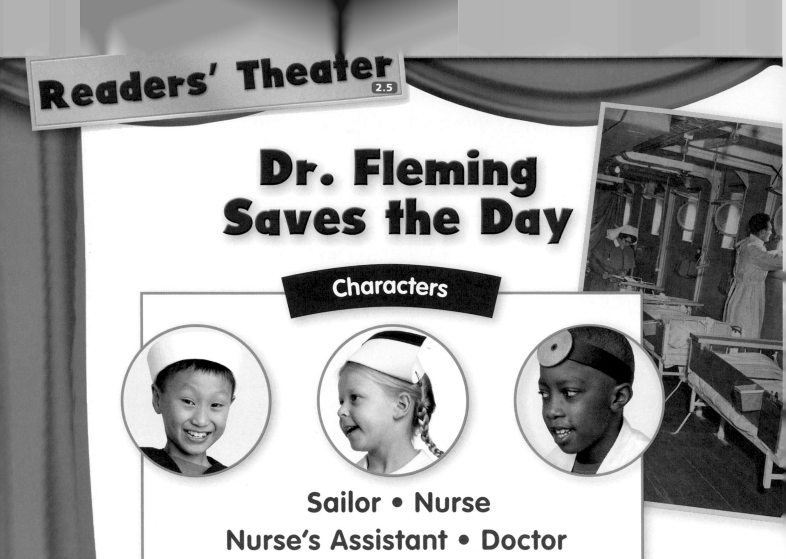

Characters

**Sailor • Nurse
Nurse's Assistant • Doctor**

Narrator: It is 1942 during World War II. A sailor knocks on the door of the American navy hospital.

Sailor: Oh, my tooth! This pain is awful!

Nurse: Come right in. I will get the doctor.

Nurse's Assistant: Here, sit down in this chair.

Sailor: I hope the doctor can help me. I hope he does not pull out my tooth!

Nurse's Assistant: Do not worry! Wait to see what the doctor says. He might say you need a little penicillin.

Sailor: Penny what?

Nurse's Assistant: (laughing) Penicillin. It is new. Doctors use it to kill harmful germs called *bacteria*.

Nurse: (walking into the room) The doctor will be here in a moment. He is with another patient.

Sailor: I hope he gets here soon. This tooth really hurts!

Nurse: Try to relax. You might need some penicillin.

Sailor: That is the second time I have heard about penicillin. I do not know anything about this medicine. Is it safe? Where did it come from?

Nurse's Assistant: Do not worry. It is perfectly safe.

Nurse: Absolutely safe. Penicillin was discovered several years ago by a doctor named Alexander Fleming.

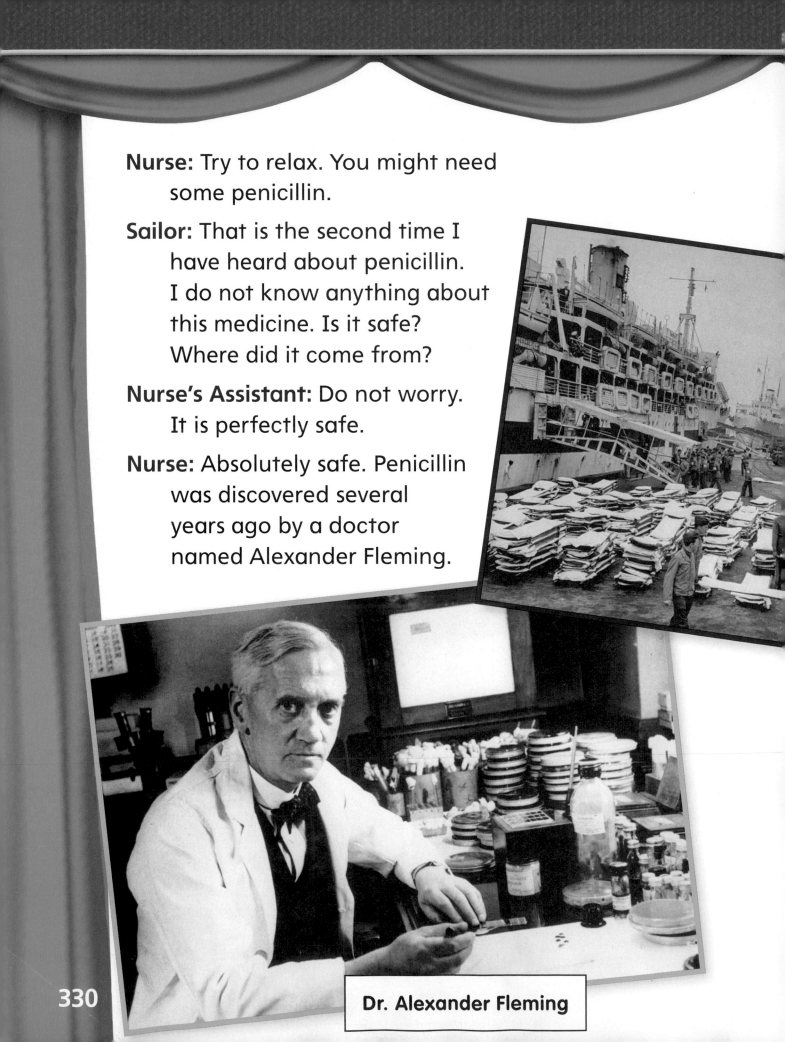

Dr. Alexander Fleming

Narrator: The ship's doctor enters the room. He is carrying a dentist's tray.

Doctor: Hello, Sailor. I understand you have a terrible toothache.

Sailor: Hello, Doctor. I was afraid you might have to pull out my tooth. Now I am hoping that this new medicine called penicillin might help me.

Doctor: Well, it just might. First, we have to see what is causing the problem. Open your mouth, please.

Narrator: The doctor looks inside the sailor's mouth and examines the tooth.

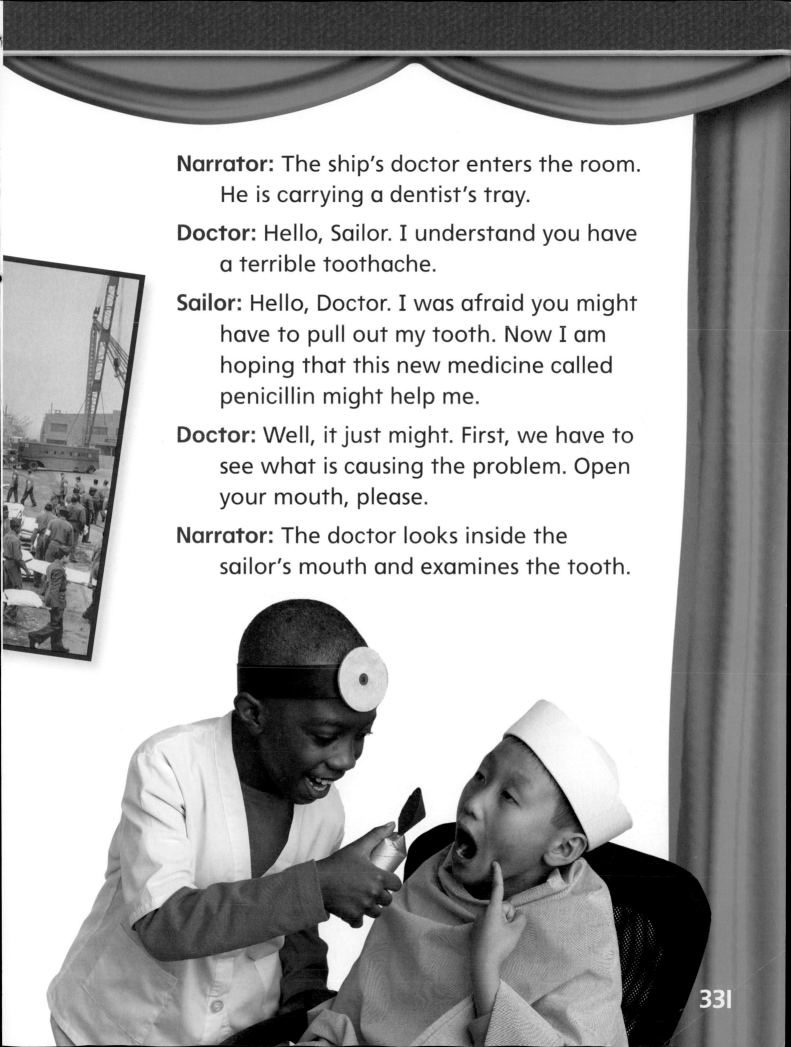

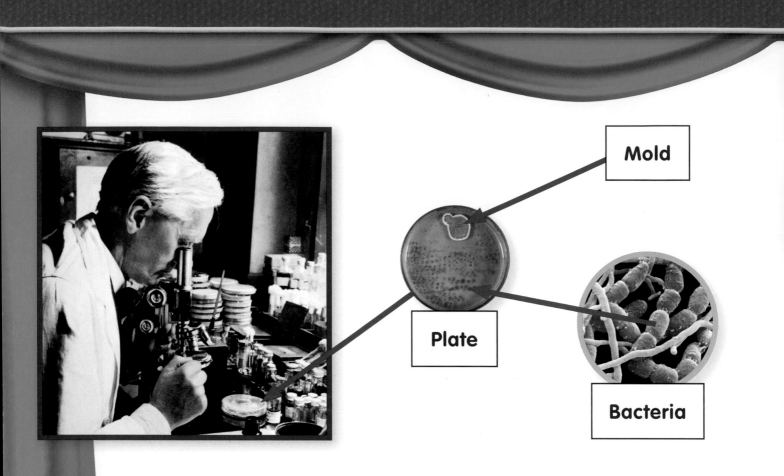

Mold

Plate

Bacteria

Doctor: Let me tell you a little bit about penicillin. Alexander Fleming discovered penicillin by accident.

Narrator: The doctor tells the sailor how Fleming put some bacteria on a plate. He studied them for two weeks. One day he saw some mold that had accidentally grown on the plate.

Sailor: What happened to the bacteria?

Doctor: Well, some bacteria still grew on the plate. But the bacteria near the mold had died! Mold killed the bacteria.

Nurse: So the mold was turned into a medicine called penicillin.

Doctor: Nurse, will you please get me some penicillin for this young man?

Sailor: You mean you will not have to pull out my tooth?

Doctor: Not at all. The penicillin will fight the bacteria. You will be better in no time!

Sailor: Thank you, Doctor. And thanks to Alexander Fleming. He saved the day!

Nurse's Assistant: (laughing) And your tooth!

Write About It! How did Alexander Fleming make the world a better place?

2.5 Students understand the importance of individual action and character and explain how heroes from long ago and the recent past have made a difference in others' lives.

Artists Are Special

Vocabulary

artist

What would the world be like without pictures? What would the world be like without stories or music? An **artist** paints, writes, dances, performs, or makes music. An artist brings beauty into our world.

Diego Rivera was a famous artist. He liked to paint pictures about life in Mexico. Rivera used bright colors to show how he felt.

Diego Rivera

Mary Cassatt was also a famous artist. She painted many pictures of mothers and their children.

Mary Cassatt

Pablo Picasso was another famous artist. He liked to paint pictures about life too. Often his paintings did not look real. Picasso painted this picture of himself.

Pablo Picasso

 What kind of pictures did Diego Rivera paint?

335

Writers and Artists

"Follow the Yellow Brick Road." You may have heard these words. They were in the movie, *The Wizard of Oz*. The story was written by L. Frank Baum.

Children loved reading Baum's stories. Many wrote him letters asking him to write more stories. He wrote 14 Oz books in all.

L. Frank Baum

Patricia Polacco writes books for children. Polacco was not a very good student when she was young. Then a special teacher helped her. Ever since then Polacco has loved to draw and write stories.

Patricia Polacco

Tomie dePaola also writes books for children. He knew he wanted to be an artist and a writer when he was only four years old! DePaola wants his books to make a difference in a child's life.

What did Tomie dePaola know when he was four years old?

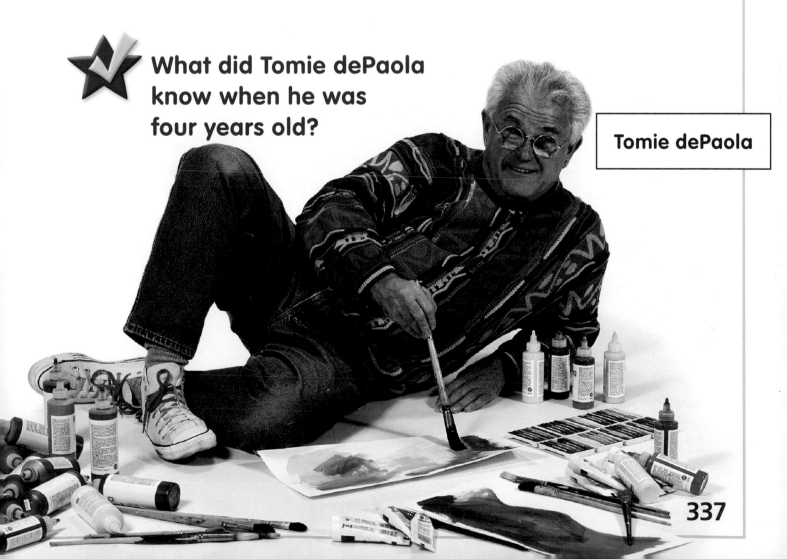

Tomie dePaola

337

Dancers and Musicians

Dancers and musicians make our lives better. They can make us feel happy and forget our troubles.

Isadora Duncan was a dancer. Duncan used natural movements in her dancing. Many people say Duncan invented modern dance.

Gregory Hines was a great tap dancer. He learned to dance before he was three years old. He was also an actor and singer.

Isadora Duncan

Gregory Hines

Long ago a six-year-old boy amazed people with his music. He played the piano for kings. His name was Wolfgang Amadeus Mozart.

Like Mozart, Vanessa Mae began to play the piano at a very young age. Then she learned to play the violin when she was only five years old. Today she plays her violin all around the world.

Wolfgang Amadeus Mozart

How can music and dance help us?

Vanessa Mae

339

Singers

Alicia Keys sings and plays the piano. She took many singing classes in school. She was a very good student and loved hip-hop music. She became famous after singing on Oprah Winfrey's TV show.

Alicia Keys

Charlotte Church is a classical singer. She made her first album when she was only twelve years old. Now Church sings all over the world.

Charlotte Church

Carlos Santana was born in Mexico. His father showed him how to play the guitar. Then he moved to California and started a band. His band was made up of black, white, and Hispanic singers and musicians.

 Who is your favorite singer? How does their music make you feel?

Lesson Review

Big Idea

1. What does an artist do?

2. What can people learn from Patricia Polacco's struggles in school?

3. **Compare and Contrast** Choose any two artists from the lesson. Tell how they are alike and different.

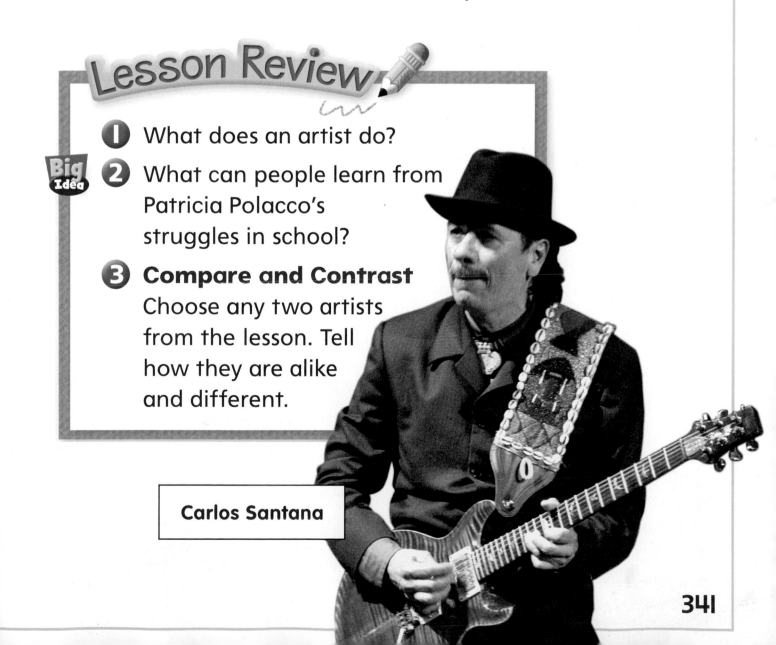

Carlos Santana

Primary Sources

2.5

Understanding Drawings

A sketch is an unfinished drawing someone makes on a piece of paper. This is an original sketch Dr. Seuss drew for his book *The Cat in the Hat*. This sketch is about 50 years old.

Look Closely

- What did Dr. Seuss use to draw this sketch?
- What do you think the cat is saying?

This sketch became pages 6 and 7 in The Cat in the Hat.

This sketch and other drawings by Dr. Seuss are kept at a special place so they will not be torn or damaged.

Dr. Seuss drawing the Grinch

Primary Source Review

1 What is a sketch?

2 Why is it important to keep this sketch in a special place?

3 Why do you think Dr. Seuss drew the cat so silly?

2.5 Students understand the importance of individual action and character and explain how heroes from long ago and the recent past have made a difference in others' lives.

Leaders for Freedom

Vocabulary

slavery

Long ago when Abraham Lincoln was President, there was a war between our states. The war was about **slavery**. Slavery is one person taking away another person's freedom.

President Lincoln was against slavery. He wrote an order that gave freedom to enslaved people in the South. Read what Lincoln said about slavery.

Abraham Lincoln with soldiers

Using Primary Sources

❝If slavery is not wrong, then nothing is wrong. I cannot remember when I did not so think and feel.❞

— Abraham Lincoln

Sitting Bull was a Lakota Indian chief. Like Lincoln, Sitting Bull also knew the importance of being free. Long ago many Native Americans were forced off their land. The government wanted to make room for white people.

Sitting Bull knew this was not fair. He had the courage to fight for his people.

 **What is slavery?**

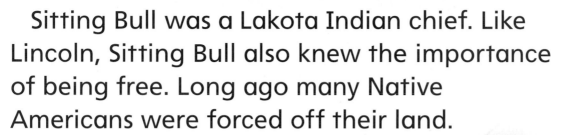

Sitting Bull

345

Speaking Out

Americans often speak out for what they think is right. Susan B. Anthony did this. For many years women were not allowed to vote.

Susan B. Anthony worked hard to change the law so that women could vote. She led marches and gave speeches. She believed that America would be a better place if all people were treated equally.

Susan B. Anthony

Rosa Parks lived in Montgomery, Alabama. Years ago many states had unfair laws. Black people had to give up their seats to white people on crowded buses. One day Rosa Parks did not give up her seat. Police took her to jail.

Mrs. Rosa Parks

Dr. Martin Luther King, Jr., worked with Rosa Parks. He told the people of Montgomery to stop riding buses until the unfair law was changed. People walked to work or school for one whole year. Finally the law was changed.

 What unfair law was changed in Montgomery?

Dr. Martin Luther King, Jr.

Working for Fairness

Cesar Chavez and Dolores Huerta worked together to make life better for farm workers. Laws said that farm workers did not have to be treated the same as other workers. They had to work long hours and were paid very little money. Cesar Chavez and Dolores Huerta gave speeches and led marches to change these laws.

Today Dolores Huerta still works to help others. She gives speeches about treating women fairly.

Cesar Chavez

Dolores Huerta

Long ago our country was at war with Japan. Japanese American citizens were not treated fairly. Some Japanese Americans were forced to leave their homes. Others, like Minoru Yasui, were not allowed to stay out late or travel at night.

One night Yasui decided to stay out late. He was arrested and spent one year in jail. When Minoru Yasui got out of jail he fought to have unfair laws changed. He helped people of all colors to be treated equally.

Minoru Yasui

 How did Minoru Yasui work for fairness?

A Japanese American family is forced to leave home.

349

Many Ways to Be a Hero

Jackie Robinson was a great baseball player. He lived during a time when black players were not allowed to play on the same team with white players. He knew this was wrong.

Robinson became the first black baseball player to play on a white team. He showed great courage. He spoke out about unfair treatment and helped others work for equality.

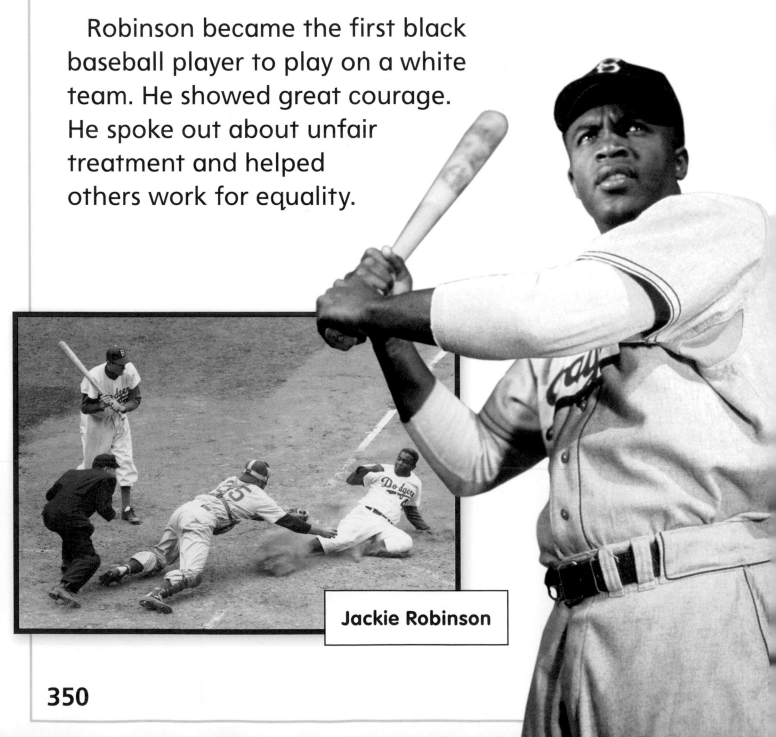

Jackie Robinson

Aung San Suu Kyi lives in Myanmar (Burma). In her country the people are not free to do as they choose. Aung San Suu Kyi knows that this is wrong. She works every day to help make Myanmar a free country.

In 1991 Suu Kyi won the Nobel Peace Prize for her hard work. Today Suu Kyi leads the people in her country to fight for freedom in peaceful ways.

Aung San Suu Kyi

 Why do you think Jackie Robinson is a hero?

Lesson Review

1. What did Lincoln think of slavery?

Big Idea 2. How is Aung San Suu Kyi making our world a better place?

3. **Make Predictions** How might your life be different if you were not free?

A Lakota Child

Meet Winona. She lived in America long ago. She belonged to a Native American group called the Lakota. Read to find out more about Winona's life.

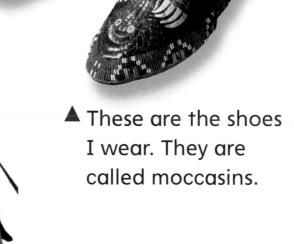

▲ These are the shoes I wear. They are called moccasins.

352

My grandmother made this dress out of buffalo skin. I only wear it on very special days! ▶

◀ When I was a baby, my mom carried me in this cradle.

▲ This is my home, at least for now! When the buffalo move, so will my family.

Write About It!

What do you wear on special days?

LOG ON For more about the Lakota, visit:

www.macmillanmh.com/ss/ca/dayinthelife

A Hero from India

Mohandas K. Gandhi was born in India. He is known as a hero to all the world. Another hero, Martin Luther King, Jr., used Gandhi's method of peacefully fighting for freedom.

Gandhi as a young lawyer

As a young man Gandhi became a lawyer. He moved to South Africa where he found out that Indians and black South Africans were treated unfairly. Gandhi knew this was wrong.

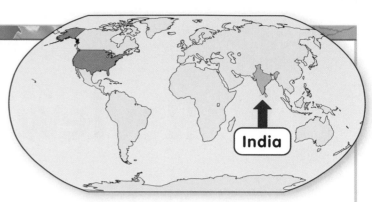

India

Later Gandhi moved home to India. India was ruled by Great Britain. Gandhi believed the Indian people should be free to rule their own country.

He taught the Indian people how to fight for freedom in a peaceful way. He told them not to buy clothes from Great Britain. He showed them how to make their own clothes. In 1947 people in India finally won their freedom.

Ghandi making clothes

Talk About It! What are some ways you can speak up peacefully for fairness?

Review

Cause and Effect

Dr. Martin Luther King, Jr., was a minister. He believed that people of all colors should be treated the same way. Dr. King taught people how to fight for their rights in peaceful ways. Many unfair laws were changed because of the work of Dr. Martin Luther King, Jr.

1 What effect did Dr. Martin Luther King, Jr.'s work have?

2 How was Dr. Martin Luther King, Jr., a cause?

Use these words to finish the sentences.

inventor   Internet   courage

3 Doing something even when you are afraid is called _____.

4 A person who makes something for the very first time is an _____.

5 The _____ is a network of information from all over the world.

Critical Thinking

6 How did Marie Curie's discovery of radium help people?

7 Name some ways that one person can make a difference.

Write About It! **8** Today we have laws that say people of all colors must be treated equally. List reasons why you think this is fair.

Critical Thinking Skills   Classify

Look at the pictures below.

Firefighters

Dancer

Military man

Singer

Police officer

Guitar player

1 Find the picture of the police officer. Now find two other pictures that are like the police officer. What could you name that group?

A   Teachers

B   Scientists

C   Everyday Heroes

D   Artists

2 How are the other three pictures alike?

A   They are all inventors.

B   They are all artists.

C   They are all volunteers.

D   They are all hospital workers.

3 What could you name that group?

A   Teachers

B   Scientists

C   Everyday Heroes

D   Artists

Many Special People Mobile

1 Draw pictures of special people on index cards.

2 On the back of the pictures, write about how each person made our world a better place to live.

3 Attach the pictures to a coat hanger with yarn.

4 Share your mobile with your class.

"Abraham Lincoln cared about freedom. He was a great President."

Read More About the Big Idea

To learn more about special people, you can read one of these books.

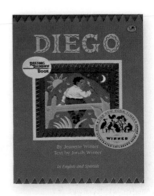

For help with the Big Idea activity, visit:

www.macmillanmh.com/ss/ca/launchpad

Reference Section Contents

Holidays

Celebrate Holidays

We celebrate holidays every year. These special days help us honor important people, events, or other things we care about.

Thanksgiving

Thanksgiving is celebrated on the fourth Thursday in November. On this day we remember the feast shared by the Pilgrims and the Native Americans. We share a meal with family and friends. We give thanks for what we have.

Activity

Create a Thanksgiving Class Collage

- Draw a picture of something you are thankful for.
- Write a label under your picture.
- Paste your picture, along with others, onto a large sheet of paper.

New Year's Day

In the United States we celebrate New Year's Day on January I. Not everyone celebrates a new year on the same day. The Chinese New Year is celebrated in January or February. The Jewish New Year is celebrated in September or October. New Years can be celebrated with parades, fireworks, dancing, and special foods.

Chinese New Year parade

Activity

Make a New Year Banner

- **Fold three sheets of paper in half.**
- **Draw pictures of three kinds of New Year celebrations.**
- **Hang the pictures on a string.**

Martin Luther King, Jr., Day

Martin Luther King, Jr., Day is celebrated on the third Monday in January. We celebrate this holiday with parades and speeches.

Dr. Martin Luther King, Jr., worked hard to change laws that were unfair to African Americans. He gave speeches and led marches. On this day we remember his dream for all people to live together in peace.

I dream that all people have food to eat.

I dream that people are kind to each other all over the world.

Activity

Write about Your Dreams

- **Cut out two large cloud shapes.**
- **Write a dream that you have for the world on each cloud.**

Presidents' Day

Presidents' Day is on the third Monday in February. On this day we honor the work of two Presidents, George Washington and Abraham Lincoln.

Schools, banks, and many offices are closed to show respect for these two great American leaders.

Activity

Make a President Postage Stamp

- **Draw a picture of President Washington or Lincoln.**
- **Add a design to the stamp.**
- **Turn the stamp over.**
- **Write a few sentences about that President.**

Cesar Chavez Day

Cesar Chavez Day is celebrated on March 31. Cesar Chavez made life better for farm workers. He worked hard to make sure they were treated fairly. On this day we celebrate his life by doing service work for our communities. We clean up parks or plant community gardens.

Activity

Write a Service Work Song

- Write words about service work that helps your community.
- Think of a tune you know.
- Put the words to the tune.
- Share your song with your class.

I pick up trash and cans,

From beaches and from land,

I think of Cesar Chavez

And I want to give a hand!

Earth Day

Some people celebrate Earth Day on March 21 and others celebrate on April 22. On Earth Day we take time to learn about ways we can keep our planet clean and healthy. Many people celebrate by planting trees or seeds, recycling, and cleaning up trash.

Activity

Make an Earth Day Mobile

- Label a strip of paper "Earth Day."
- Staple the strip into a circle.
- Draw three pictures of things to do on Earth Day.
- Tie yarn to the top of each picture.
- Staple the yarn to the paper circle.
- Hang up high.

Cinco de Mayo

Cinco de Mayo means "fifth of May" in Spanish. This holiday celebrates the day in 1862 when Mexico won a hard battle with France. It celebrates the courage of the Mexican Army. This holiday is celebrated with parades, parties, and speeches.

Activity

Create a Cinco de Mayo Poster

- Write a Spanish saying on your poster, such as "¡Viva la libertad!" (Long live liberty!)
- Draw pictures of a Cinco de Mayo celebration and the Mexican flag.

Mother's Day and Father's Day

Mother's Day is the second Sunday in May. Father's Day is the third Sunday in June. People send cards, flowers, or do something special to show love for their parents on these days.

I love you. Thank you for taking care of me.

Love, Evan

Activity

Make a Card

- **Fold a sheet of construction paper in half.**
- **Draw a picture of your mother, father, or guardian on the front.**
- **Write sentences that tell how you feel about this person on the inside.**

Memorial Day

Memorial Day is celebrated on the last Monday in May. On this day we show respect for the soldiers who died in our country's wars. Many people celebrate this holiday by going to parades or visiting war memorials.

We remember our heroes.

Activity

Make a Memorial Day Wreath

- **Make a flower out of colorful tissue paper.**
- **Attach or paste the flower to a piece of cardboard shaped like a wreath.**
- **Attach a message under the wreath.**

Independence Day

Independence Day, or the Fourth of July, honors our country's birthday. We remember that on July 4, 1776, we declared our freedom. We celebrate with parades and fireworks to show that we are proud to be Americans.

Activity

Play a Fourth of July Matching Game

- **Choose Fourth of July symbols such as the Liberty Bell, flag, bald eagle, or fireworks.**
- **Draw the symbols on index cards.**
- **Write matching words that name the symbols on other index cards.**
- **Play the matching game with a partner.**

THE UNITED STATES

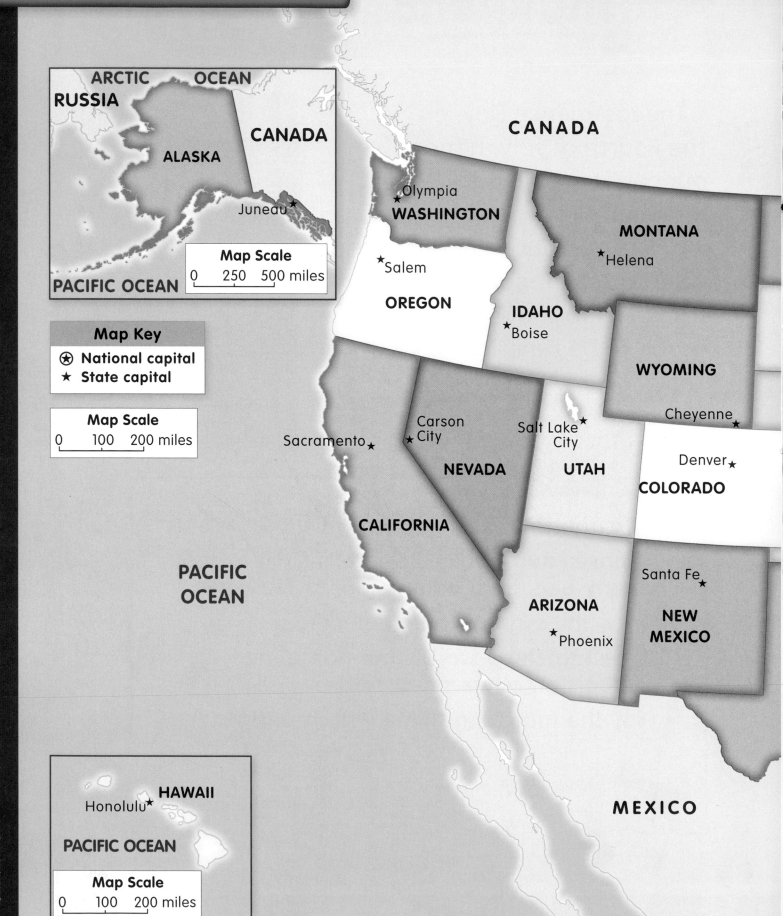

ARCTIC OCEAN

RUSSIA

CANADA

ALASKA

Juneau ★

PACIFIC OCEAN

Map Scale
0   250   500 miles

Map Key
⊛ National capital
★ State capital

Map Scale
0   100   200 miles

CANADA

Olympia ★
WASHINGTON

★ Salem

OREGON

MONTANA
★ Helena

IDAHO
★ Boise

WYOMING

Cheyenne ★

Carson
City ★

Salt Lake ★
City

Sacramento ★

NEVADA

UTAH

Denver ★
COLORADO

PACIFIC
OCEAN

CALIFORNIA

Santa Fe ★

ARIZONA

★ Phoenix

NEW
MEXICO

HAWAII
Honolulu ★

PACIFIC OCEAN

MEXICO

Map Scale
0   100   200 miles

CANADA

NORTH
DAKOTA
★Bismarck

MINNESOTA

Lake
Superior

MICHIGAN

Lake
Huron

NEW
HAMPSHIRE
VERMONT

MAINE

★Augusta

Montpelier★

★Concord
Boston

SOUTH
DAKOTA
★Pierre

St. Paul★

WISCONSIN

Lake
Michigan

Lansing★

Lake
Erie

Lake
Ontario

Albany

NEW YORK

★MASSACHUSETTS
★Providence

Madison★

Hartford★

RHODE ISLAND
CONNECTICUT

NEBRASKA

IOWA

★Des
Moines

INDIANA

OHIO

PENNSYLVANIA

Trenton★

NEW JERSEY

Lincoln★

ILLINOIS

Columbus
★

Harrisburg★

Dover
★

DELAWARE

Springfield★

Indianapolis★

Washington, D.C.

⊛

★Annapolis

Topeka★

Jefferson★
City

WEST
VIRGINIA

★Charleston

★Richmond

MARYLAND

KANSAS

Frankfort
★

VIRGINIA

MISSOURI

KENTUCKY

Nashville
★

NORTH
CAROLINA

★Raleigh

Oklahoma
City
★

TENNESSEE

ARKANSAS

Columbia
★

OKLAHOMA

Little★
Rock

ALABAMA

Atlanta
★

GEORGIA

SOUTH
CAROLINA

ATLANTIC
OCEAN

MISSISSIPPI

★Jackson

Montgomery
★

TEXAS

LOUISIANA

Austin★

Baton Rouge★

★Tallahassee

FLORIDA

THE
BAHAMAS

Gulf of Mexico

North

West ✦ East

South

CUBA

R15

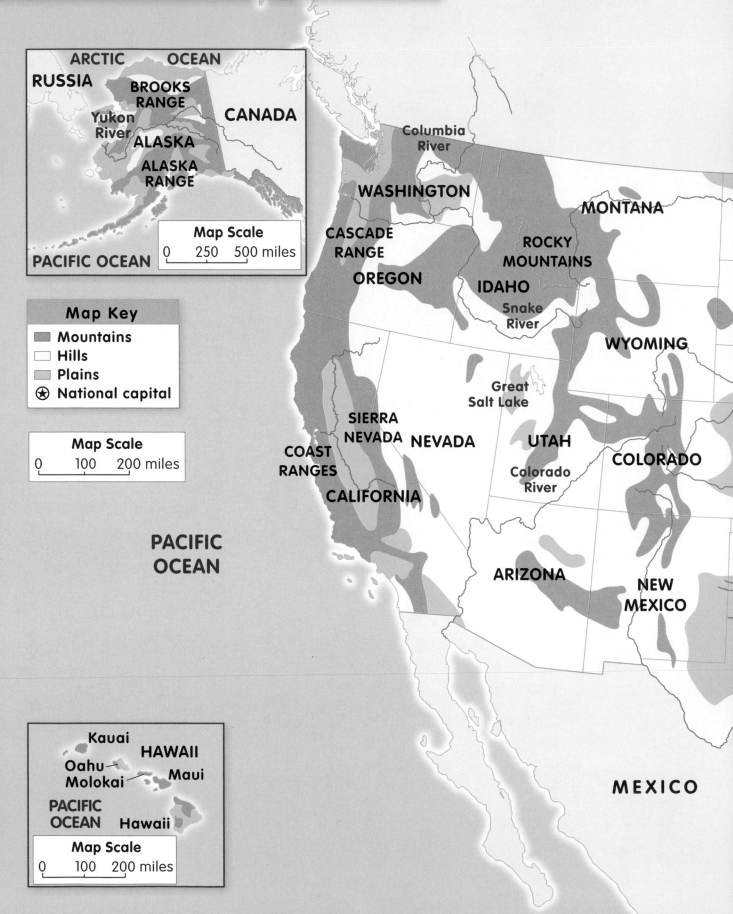

ARCTIC OCEAN

RUSSIA

BROOKS RANGE

Yukon River

CANADA

ALASKA

ALASKA RANGE

PACIFIC OCEAN

Map Scale

0   250   500 miles

Map Key

■ Mountains
□ Hills
■ Plains
⊛ National capital

Map Scale

0   100   200 miles

Columbia River

WASHINGTON

CASCADE RANGE

OREGON

MONTANA

ROCKY MOUNTAINS

IDAHO

Snake River

WYOMING

Great Salt Lake

SIERRA NEVADA

COAST RANGES

NEVADA

UTAH

COLORADO

Colorado River

CALIFORNIA

PACIFIC OCEAN

ARIZONA

NEW MEXICO

MEXICO

Kauai

HAWAII

Oahu

Molokai

Maui

PACIFIC OCEAN

Hawaii

Map Scale

0   100   200 miles

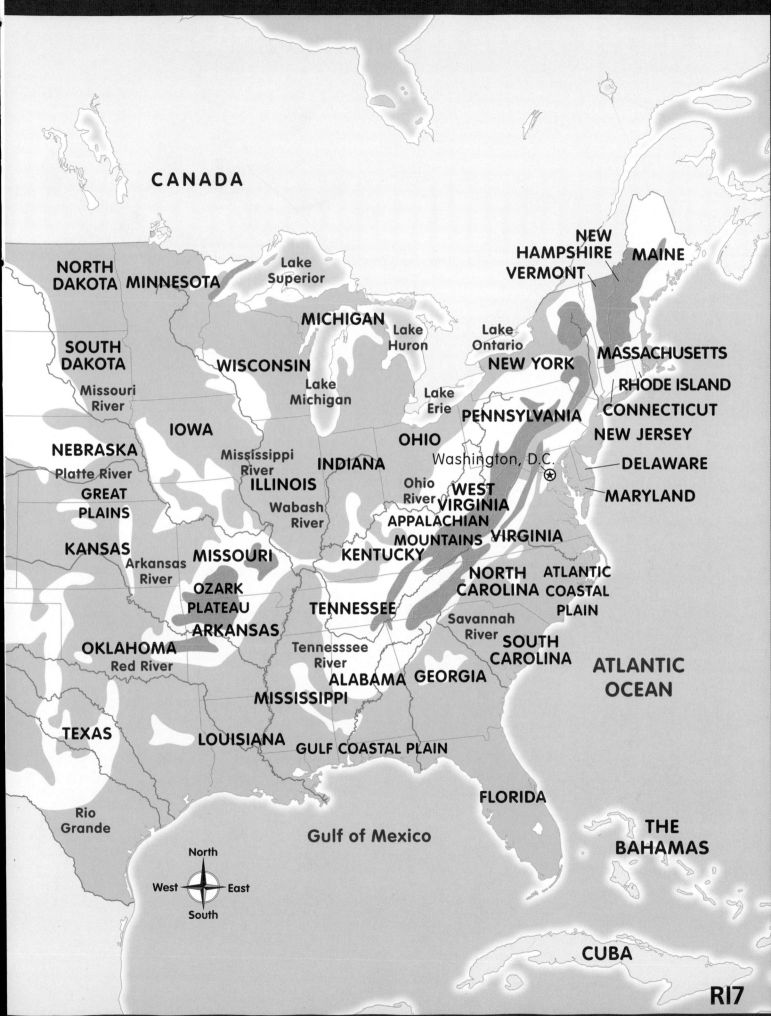

CANADA

NORTH DAKOTA   MINNESOTA
Lake Superior
MICHIGAN
Lake Huron
Lake Ontario
NEW HAMPSHIRE   MAINE
VERMONT

SOUTH DAKOTA
WISCONSIN
Lake Michigan
Lake Erie
NEW YORK
MASSACHUSETTS
RHODE ISLAND
CONNECTICUT

Missouri River
IOWA
PENNSYLVANIA
NEW JERSEY

NEBRASKA
Mississippi River
INDIANA
OHIO
Washington, D.C.
DELAWARE

Platte River
ILLINOIS
Ohio River
WEST VIRGINIA
MARYLAND

GREAT PLAINS
Wabash River
APPALACHIAN MOUNTAINS
VIRGINIA

KANSAS
Arkansas River
MISSOURI
KENTUCKY
NORTH CAROLINA
ATLANTIC COASTAL PLAIN

OZARK PLATEAU
TENNESSEE
SOUTH CAROLINA

OKLAHOMA
ARKANSAS
Savannah River
ATLANTIC OCEAN

Red River
Tennesssee River
ALABAMA   GEORGIA

TEXAS
MISSISSIPPI
LOUISIANA
GULF COASTAL PLAIN

Rio Grande
Gulf of Mexico
FLORIDA
THE BAHAMAS

North
West — East
South

CUBA

R17

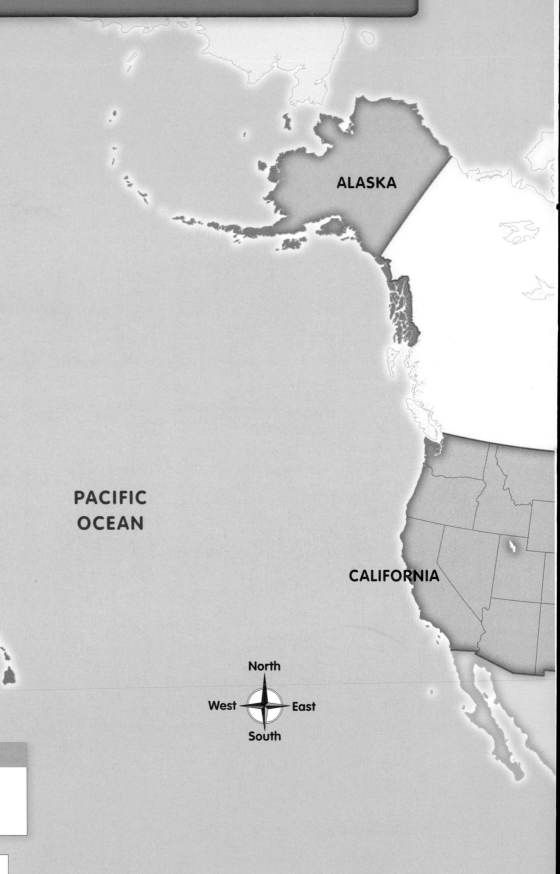

ALASKA

PACIFIC
OCEAN

CALIFORNIA

HAWAII

North

West ⊕ East

South

Map Key
▢ Country border
▬ State borders
⊛ National capital

Map Scale
0   250   500 miles

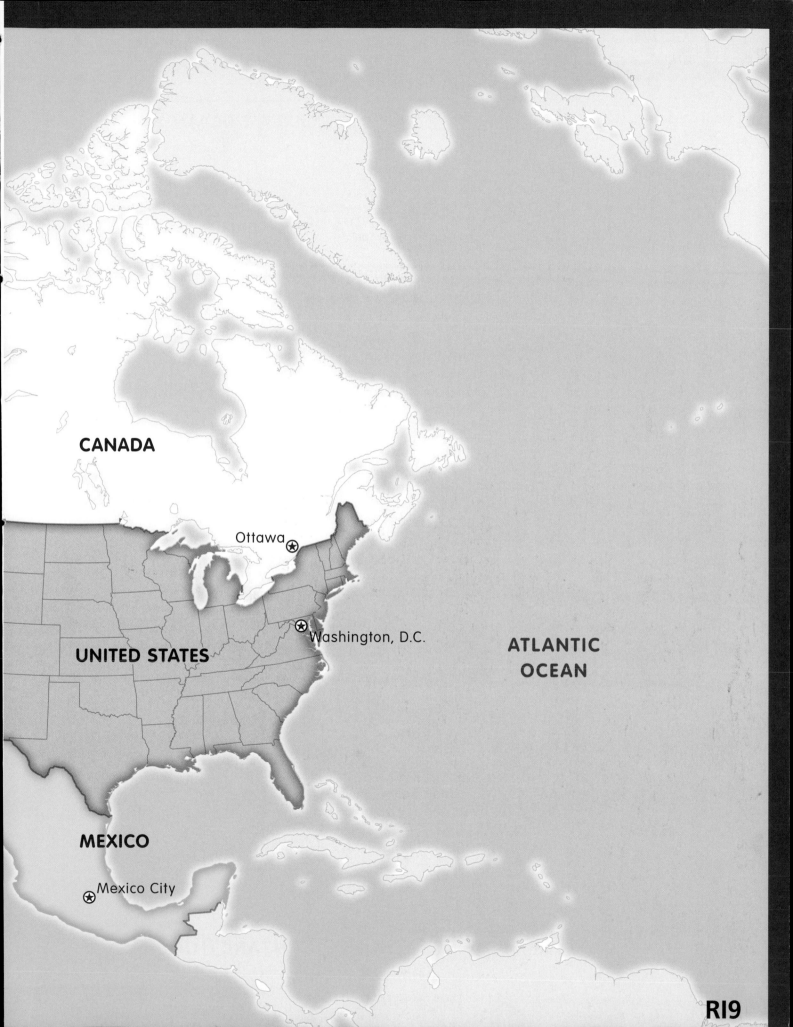

CANADA

UNITED STATES

MEXICO

Ottawa ✪

Washington, D.C. ✪

ATLANTIC
OCEAN

✪ Mexico City

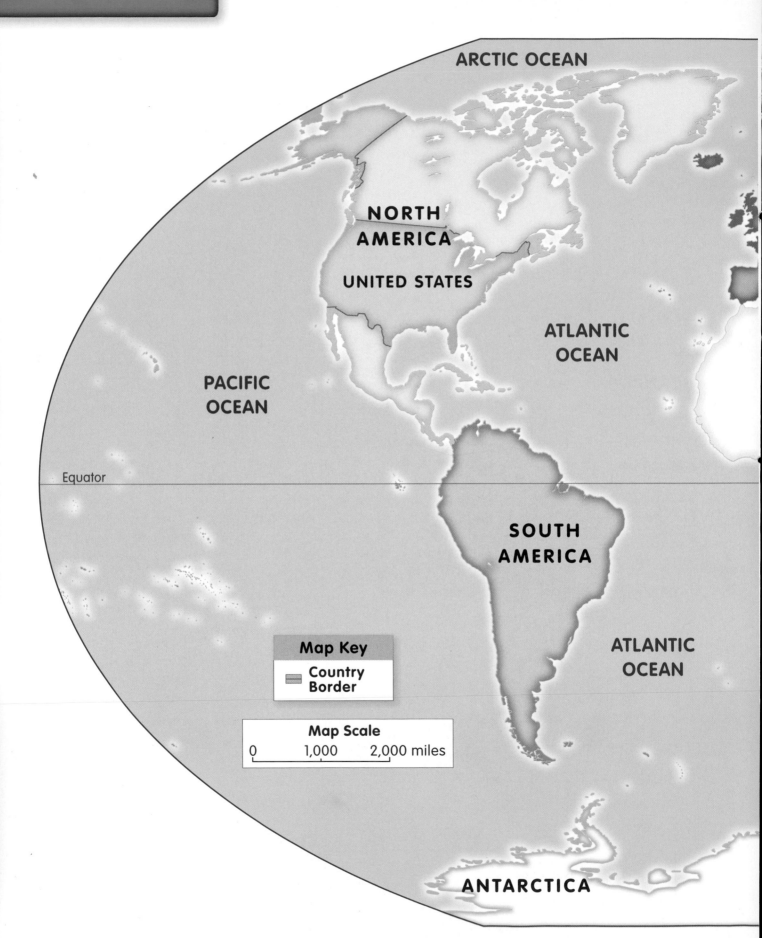

ARCTIC OCEAN

NORTH AMERICA

UNITED STATES

ATLANTIC OCEAN

PACIFIC OCEAN

Equator

SOUTH AMERICA

ATLANTIC OCEAN

Map Key

Country Border

Map Scale

0   1,000   2,000 miles

ANTARCTICA

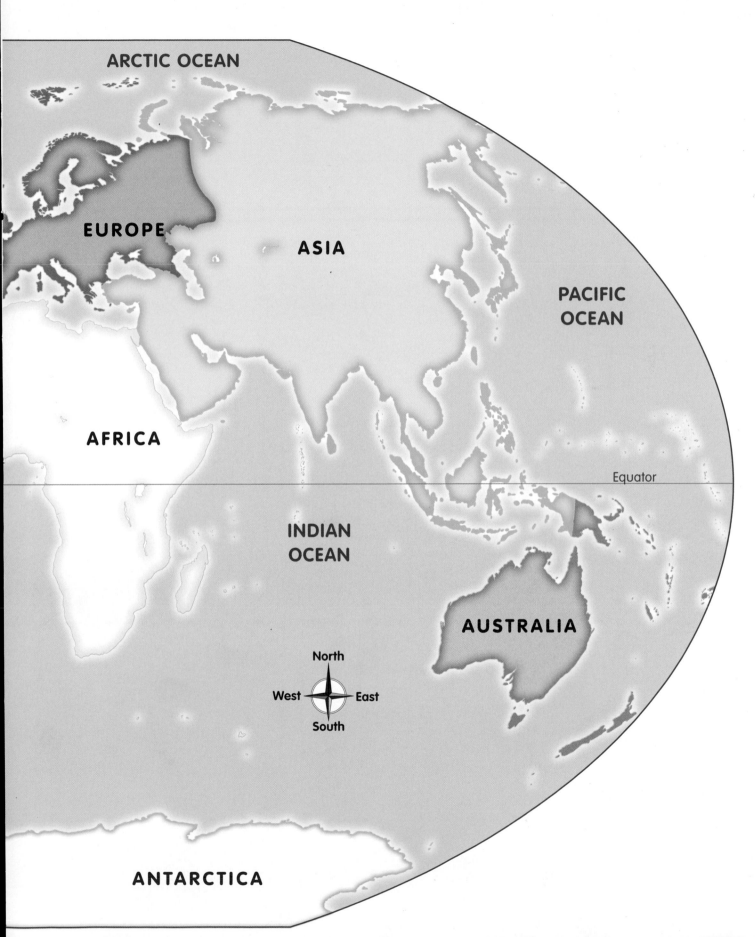

ARCTIC OCEAN

EUROPE

ASIA

PACIFIC
OCEAN

AFRICA

Equator

INDIAN
OCEAN

AUSTRALIA

North

West — East

South

ANTARCTICA

NORTH AMERICA

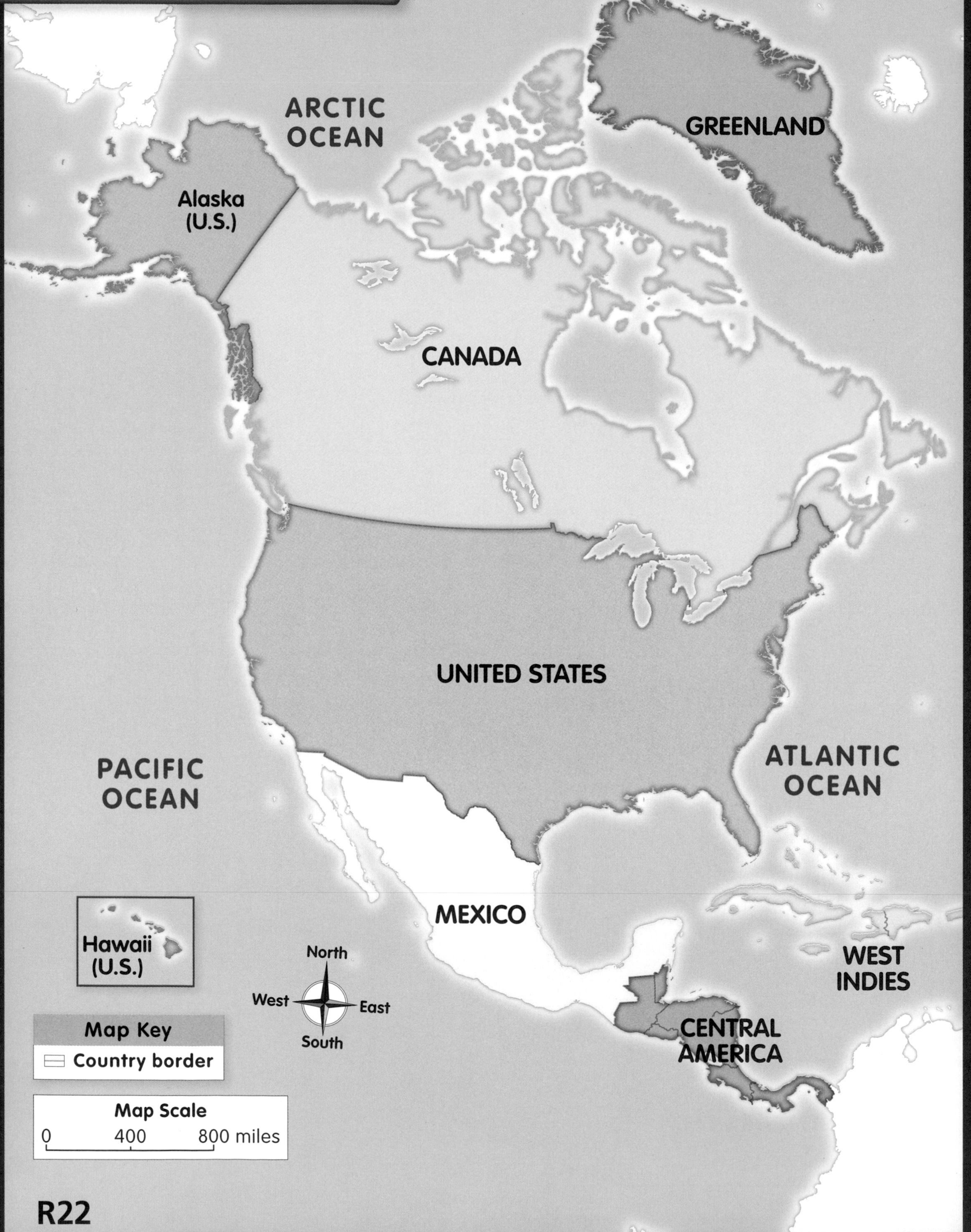

ARCTIC OCEAN
GREENLAND
Alaska (U.S.)
CANADA
UNITED STATES
PACIFIC OCEAN
ATLANTIC OCEAN
MEXICO
Hawaii (U.S.)
North
West
East
South
WEST INDIES
CENTRAL AMERICA
Map Key
Country border
Map Scale
0
400
800 miles

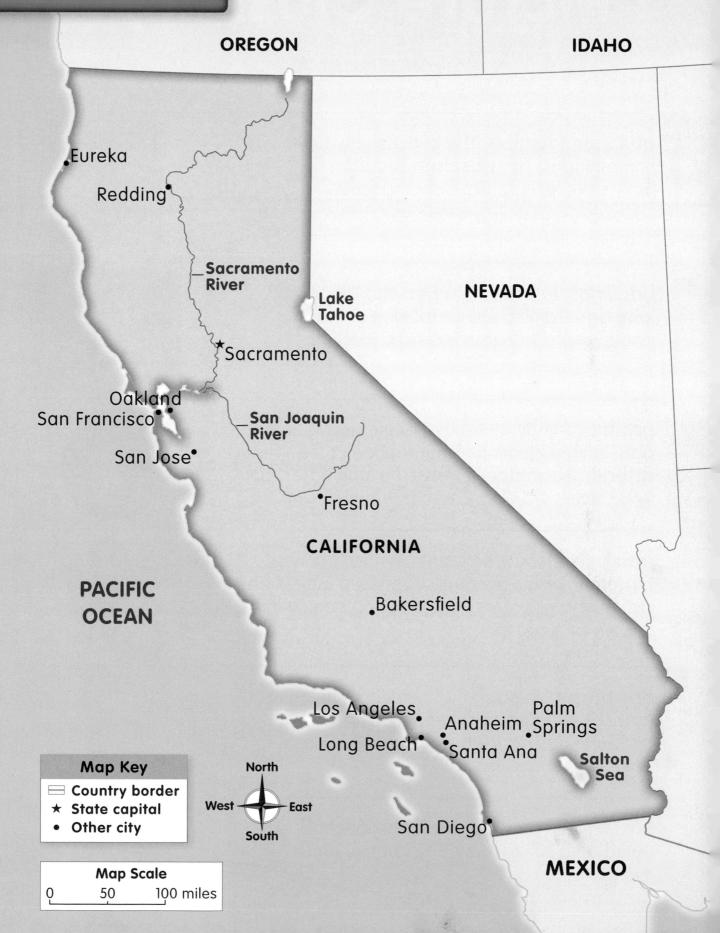

CALIFORNIA

OREGON

IDAHO

Eureka

Redding

Sacramento River

Lake Tahoe

NEVADA

★ Sacramento

Oakland
San Francisco

San Joaquin River

San Jose

Fresno

CALIFORNIA

PACIFIC OCEAN

Bakersfield

Los Angeles

Palm Springs

Anaheim

Long Beach

Santa Ana

Salton Sea

San Diego

MEXICO

Map Key
▭ Country border
★ State capital
• Other city

North
West — East
South

Map Scale
0   50   100 miles

R23

absolute location The exact spot where something is. The **absolute location** of Gary's house is 12 Elm Street. (page 86)

ancestor A family member who lived long, long ago. Tamika enjoys looking at old photographs of her **ancestors**. (page 20)

artifact Things made by people a long time ago, such as tools and handmade crafts. This **artifact** was made in Mexico a long time ago. (page 196)

artist A person who paints, writes, dances, performs, or makes music. Vanessa Mae is an **artist** who plays her violin to bring beauty into the world. (page 334)

B

bar graph A graph that uses bars to show and compare information. The **bar graph** shows things recycled in Mrs. Cody's class. (page 96)

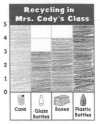

bill An idea for a new law. The lawmakers voted on a **bill** to make the country better. (page 164)

border A line that separates one state or country from another. We crossed the **border** between California and Oregon on our family vacation. (page 56)

browser buttons An Internet tool. Click the "Back" **browser button** to go back to the first Web site. (page 326)

C

calendar A chart that shows the 12 months of the year. Janet looked at the **calendar** to find out when the school bake sale starts. (page 36)

capital The city where the people of our government work. The city of Sacramento is the **capital** of California. (page 170)

Capitol The building where our lawmakers, or Congress work. This is the **Capitol** in Washington D.C. (page 171)

cause A person, thing, or event that makes something happen. Charles Drew was the **cause** of finding a new way to store blood. (page 304)

chapter heading The name of a chapter in a book. The **chapter heading** of this chapter is "Baskets." (page 137)

Baskets

The Miwok Indians make beautiful baskets. The baskets are used for many different things. This basket is used to cook food.

choice Something picked from a number of things. Bill makes a **choice** between eating an apple or a banana. (page 231)

citizen A member of a community, state, or country. To become a United States **citizen**, you must promise to obey the laws. (page 63)

classify To put things that are alike into groups. We can **classify** the people in this photo as "soccer players." (page 310)

coast Land that runs along the water. Emily's family drove along the **coast** of California. (page 101)

community A place where people live, work, and have fun together. I live in the **community** of Burlingame, California. (page 90)

compare To find out how things are alike. When I **compare** the guitar players, I can see that they are all wearing black jackets. (page 8)

compass rose A symbol on a map that points to the letters N, S, E, and W. The **compass rose** shows me that California is west of Nevada. (page 18)

Congress All of our country's lawmakers together. We saw **Congress** at work on our trip to Washington, D.C. (page 164)

Constitution A plan that tells us how to run the government. You can see the **Constitution** in Washington, D.C. (page 156)

consumer Someone who uses the goods made by a producer. This **consumer** is buying grapes. (page 275)

contrast To find out how things are different. When I **contrast** the two children, I can see that one is taller than the other. (page 8)

continent A very large piece of land. We saw kangaroos on our trip to the **continent** of Australia. (page 118)

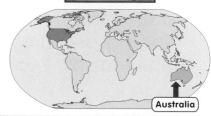

cooperate To work together. Juan and Clay **cooperate** to finish their chores faster. (page 202)

country The land and the people who live there. India is a **country** on the continent of Asia. (page 117)

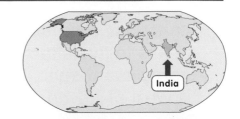

courage Doing something even when you are afraid. Firefighters need **courage** to do their jobs. (page 312)

court A building where judges work. People go to a **court** to get help if they cannot agree about a law. (page 166)

crop A group of plants grown for food. This **crop** of wheat can be used to make a lot of bread. (page 239)

culture The way a group of people live, including their food, music, and traditions. Yoga came from the **culture** of India. (page 62)

D

dairy farm A special farm for dairy cows. The milk we drink comes from the cows on **dairy farms**. (page 256)

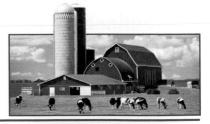

desert A hot, dry area with few plants. We brought plenty of water to drink when we drove though the **desert**. (page 99)

details More information about the main idea. Finding **details** in the story helped me understand more about what I read. (page 82)

detail

diagram A picture with labels to tell what things are. This **diagram** shows the different parts of a courtroom. (page 182)

discovery Something that is seen or found for the first time. Penicillin was a very important **discovery** made by Alexander Fleming. (page 320)

document A written or printed paper that gives information. The Declaration of Independence is an important **document** from our past. (page 160)

E

effect The thing that actually happens because of the cause. The **effect** of Charles Drew's work was a way to store blood. (page 304)

F

factory A building where things are made. This **factory** can make many jars of grape jam at one time. (page 273)

flow chart A chart that shows the order in which things happen, or flow. The second step of the **flow chart** shows dough being shaped into loaves. (page 244)

G

geography The study of the things that make up our Earth. **Geography** helps us learn about Earth. (page 74)

globe A model of Earth. Our teacher showed us the Atlantic Ocean on the **globe**. (page 74)

goods The things we buy. The people in the community buy **goods** at the store. (page 234)

government The group of people who run a community, state, or country. A community board is one part of a community **government**. (page 146)

governor The leader of a state. The **governor** is giving a speech about how to make the state better. (page 179)

grid map A map divided into squares. The courthouse is in square B4 on the **grid map**. (page 88)

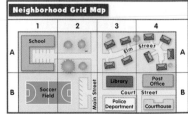

guardian A person who takes care of you like a parent. John's **guardian** reads him family letters from long ago. (page 32)

H **hero** A person who does something brave or important that helps others. A police officer is an everyday **hero**. (page 313)

hill Land that is higher than land around it, but not as high as a mountain. We walked up the **hill**. (page 98)

history The story of the past. I can learn about my family's **history** by looking at photographs. (page 2)

I **immigrant** A person who leaves one country to live in another. My great grandmother was an **immigrant** from China. (page 54)

individual One person. Nicholaus Otto was the **individual** who made the engine. (page 307)

Internet A network of information from all over the world. We can use the **Internet** to learn about many things. (page 326)

interview To ask a person questions and write down the answers. Sam **interviewed** his grandmother and Mrs. Garcia to find out how they came to California. (page 20)

inventor A person who makes something for the very first time. The Wright brothers were the **inventors** of the airplane. (page 322)

irrigation Putting water into the soil with special machines. The farmer had to use **irrigation** to water his crops because it did not rain enough. (page 266)

island A landform that has water going all the way around it. Catalina **Island** is a part of the state of California. (page 100)

J

judge A person who decides what the laws mean. **Judges** are one of the three groups who run our government. (page 162)

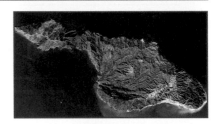

jury A group of citizens who are chosen to listen to a trial and work with the judge to decide what is fair. My mom was chosen to be on a **jury**. (page 166)

L

label The part of a diagram that tells what things are. Reading the **labels** helps you understand a diagram. (page 182)

A Courtroom

1 **Jury Box** The jury sits here to listen.
2 **Judge's Bench** The judge's desk is called a bench.
3 **Court Reporter Desk** The court reporter records, or writes, everything that is said.

4 **Witness Stand** A witness is a person who tells what they know. They promise to tell the truth.
5 **Legal Tables** The people who are on trial and their lawyers sit at these tables.
6 **Gallery** This area is where people who watch the trial sit.

lake A body of water with land all around it. We went fishing in the **lake**. (page 103)

landform The different shapes of land on Earth. This mountain is a huge **landform** in California. (page 98)

law A rule for a community or government. Some **laws** are shown on signs. (page 155)

lawmaker A person who finds out what laws citizens want to have. We voted for a **lawmaker** who will vote for laws we want to have. (page 159)

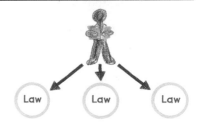

location The place or area where something is. The globe's **location** is on the cubbies. (page 84)

M

main idea What something is mostly about. The **main idea** tells you the most important part. (page 82)

main idea — Josh needed help finding things at his new school. The principal showed him where to find his new classroom. The teacher showed him where to sharpen his pencils. His new friend Anne showed him the playground behind the school.

map scale The part of a map that tells the distance between places. The **map scale** on this map shows that one inch equals 100 miles. (page 48)

Map Scale		
0	50	100 miles

mission A place where a group of church members live and work. The city of San Diego was a **mission** long ago. (page 41)

mountain The highest form of land. There is snow on the top of this **mountain**. (page 98)

N

Native Americans The first people to live in America, also called American Indians. Many **Native Americans** were forced to leave their homes by the government. (page 38)

natural resources Things in nature that are ready for people to use. Sunlight is a **natural resource**. (page 107)

needs Things that people must have to live. Food, shelter, clothing, and love are **needs**. (page 218)

O

ocean The largest body of water. We live near the Pacific **Ocean**. (page 100)

orchard A farm where fruit trees are grown. We picked apples at an apple **orchard**. (page 248)

P

pasteurize To heat to kill germs. We know that our milk has no germs in it because it has been **pasteurized**. (page 258)

peninsula A landform that has water on all sides but one. One side of a **peninsula** is part of a larger body of land. (page 101)

Pilgrim A person from England who traveled to America on a ship called the *Mayflower.* The **Pilgrims** left their country to find a better life in America. (page 42)

pioneer A person who leaves home to lead the way into a land he or she does not know. Many **pioneers** traveled in covered wagons. (page 50)

plain A flat area of land. Most **plains** are good locations for farms. (page 99)

President The leader of our country. George W. Bush is our 43rd **President.** (page 163)

problem Something you need to think about. Ann is having a **problem** deciding how to name her soccer team. (page 168)

producer Someone who makes or grows products, or goods, to sell. This farmer is a **producer** who grows grapes. (page 272)

product A good, or a thing, that is made or grown. This map shows the many food **products** grown in California. (page 262)

recycle To change a thing into something new that can be used again. Old cans can be **recycled** into new cans. (page 111)

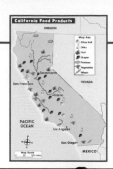

relative location Where something is compared to another thing. The **relative location** of the red house is next to the blue house. (page 87)

reuse To use again. We can **reuse** this milk carton as a bird feeder. (page 110)

river A single stream of water that flows into a larger body of water, like an ocean. We took a boat ride on the **river**. (page 102)

route A way of going from one place to another. We did not get lost because we followed a **route** on the map. (page 254)

rural A community that is located far away from a city. My uncle's farm is in a **rural** community. (page 91)

S

save To keep something to use later. I will **save** my money so I can buy a new book. (page 232)

scarce When there is not enough of something. I cannot buy a new book because my money is **scarce**. (page 232)

scientist A person who works in a special part of science. Marie Curie was a **scientist** who discovered how to use radium to cure illnesses. (page 320)

sequence The order in which things happen. The **sequence** tells what happens first, next, and last. (page 228)

service Something useful that people do for others. This doctor does a **service** by helping people when they are sick. (page 234)

settler A person who moves from one place to live in another place. The first Spanish **settlers** built a town called St. Augustine. (page 40)

shelter A place where people live. We need **shelter** to protect us from the weather. (page 230)

slavery One person taking away another person's freedom. President Lincoln believed that **slavery** was wrong. (page 344)

solve To find an answer to a problem. Ann **solved** her problem by asking her team to vote on a team name. (page 168)

state A part of a country. The **state** of Alaska is one part of the United States. (page 116)

strike To stop working. The workers at Pete's farm went on **strike** because they were not being paid enough money. (page 268)

suburban An area near a city. Many families live in this **suburban** community. (page 91)

summarize To briefly tell or write about something you have read. I can **summarize** this list by saying, "These are our classroom rules. They help us to get along." (page 152)

1. Take turns.
2. Be polite.
3. Raise your hand before you speak.
4. Clean up your work area.
5. Listen to the teacher.

Supreme Court The most important court in our country. The **Supreme Court** is located in Washington, D.C. (page 166)

T

table of contents The part of a book that tells you the name and page number of each chapter or lesson in the book. Look in the **table of contents** to find the lesson "Painting." (page 136)

tax Money paid to the government by the citizens. Police officers are paid with **tax** money from the government. (page 186)

technology The science of making things faster, easier, or better. Computer **technology** has made it easier to find information. (page 241)

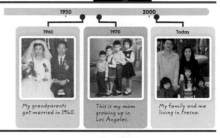

time line A line that shows the order in which things have happened. This **time line** shows the history of Li's family. (page 28)

title The name of a book. The **title** of the book is *Native American Art in California.* (page 136)

Native American Art in California

trade To give something and then get something back. The United States **trades** goods with many other countries. (page 282)

tradition A special way of doing something that is passed down over time. Eating with chopsticks is a **tradition** in my family. (page 10)

trial A meeting to decide if someone broke the law. The judge listened to both sides at the **trial**. (page 166)

U

urban The area of a city. On our class trip, we took pictures of the tall buildings in the **urban** community of San Francisco. (page 90)

URL A Web site address. This **URL** is the Web site address for the Library of Congress. (page 326)

Back   Forward   Stop

www.loc.gov

V

valley A low area between mountains or hills. We walked down to the floor of the **valley**. (page 99)

volunteer A person who works for no pay to help others. Mark is a **volunteer** who plays chess every Sunday with Mr. Jones. (page 316)

vote To choose someone or something. Citizens **vote** to choose their leaders. (page 158)

W

wants Things that people would like to have but do not need. Toys, games, and this CD player are **wants** . (page 218)

Web site A group of information that is found together in just one place on the Internet. This **Web site** is from the Library of Congress. (page 326)

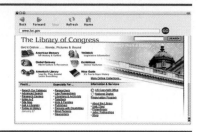

White House The building where the President lives and works. My class went on a tour of the **White House** during our trip to Washington, D.C. (page 171)

This index lists many things you can find in your book. It tells the page numbers on which they are found. The letter *m* before a page number tells you that a map is on that page.

★ Credits ★

Cover Design: Studio Montage

Maps: MapQuest

Illustration Credits: Deborah White, 4, 5; Doreen Gay-Kassel, 37; Obadinah Heavner, 76-77, 78-79; Peggy Tagel, 85; Erika LeBarre, 86; Robert Crawford, 90-91; Rachel Geswaldo, 104; Rachel Geswaldo, 111; John Hanley, 126-127; Jill Newton, 148-149; Dana Regan, 183; Ken Batelman, 215; Rachel Geswaldo, 216; Erika LeBarre, 220-221, 222-223, 224-225; Scott Gotto, 270-271; Linda Howard-Bittner, 283; Rachel Geswaldo, 296; Liz Conrad, 302-303; John Mantha, 307; Rachel Geswaldo, 360

All Photographs are by Macmillan/McGraw-Hill except as noted below:

Cover Photos: (t) Neil Gilchrist/Panoramic Images. (b) Ross Whitaker for Macmillan/McGraw-Hill. Back Cover: (bkgd) M. Angelo/CORBIS; (inset) One Mile Up/FotoSearch. Endpapers: (flag) Macmillan/McGraw-Hill; (seal) One Mile Up/Fotosearch, LLC.

iii: Ross Whittaker. iv: (c)Bettmann/CORBIS. v: Robert Glusic/Photodisc/Getty. vi: (c) Royalty-Free/CORBIS. vii: Comstock Production Dept/Comstock Images/Alamy images. viii: (c) Ed Bock/CORBIS. G2-G3: Wolfgang Kaehler/CORBIS. G3: Courtesy of Steve Cunha. G4: (l) (c)Mark E. Gibson/Gibson Stock Photography; (r) (c)Bill Ross/CORBIS. G5: (t) (c)Royalty-Free/CORBIS; (bl) Shaun Cunningham/Alamy Images; (br) Craig Steven Thrasher/Alamy Images. G10: Austin Brown/Stone/Getty Images. G14: Bryan Allen/CORBIS. 1: (bkgd) Bettmann/CORBIS. 2: (b) (c)Topham/The Image Works . 3: (tl) Underwood Archives; (r) Carl Iwasaki/Time Life Pictures/Getty Images; (bl) (c)Bettmann/CORBIS. 6: (all photos) The Granger Collection, New York. 7: (both) Lewis Wickes Hine/(c)Bettmann/CORBIS. 9: (t) (c)Minnesota Historical Society/CORBIS; (b) (c)Ariel Skelley/CORBIS. 10: (c)Royalty Free/CORBIS. 11: (l) Ken Karp for MMH; (r) Alfredo Trombetta/(c)Alinari Archives/CORBIS. 12: (c)Phil Schermeister/CORBIS. 13: (t) (c)David Schmidt/Masterfile; (t inset) Brian Leatart/Foodpix. 14: (b) (c)Syracuse Newspapers/Albert Fanning/The Image Works . 15: (t) (c)Charles & Josette Lenars/CORBIS. 16: (c)Royalty-Free/CORBIS. 16: H. Armstrong Roberts/Retrofile.com. 17: tThe Library of Congress. 21: (t) Artville/Photodisc/Getty Images; (b) Bluford W. Muir/(c)CORBIS. 22: Underwood Archives. 23: (t) Bettmann/Corbis; (b) Barnaby's Studios Ltd./Mary Evans Picture Library . 24: (l) Ben Wiedel-Kaufmann/Janine Wiedel Photolibrary/Alamy Images; (r) George Pickow/Hulton Archive/Getty Images. 25: (c)CORBIS. 26: Special Collections Department U.S.C Library. 26-27: (c) AP-Wide World Photos. 27: (l) (c)Royalty-Free/CORBIS; (r) C Squared Studios/Getty Images. 28: (r) Rafael and Alzira Simas/Marlene Simas Angeja. 29: (l,r) Private Collection. 30: Fred Ramage/Hulton Archive/Getty Images. 31: (t) (c)Bettmann/CORBIS; (b) (c)Kevin Dodge/Masterfile. 32: Wallace Kirkland/Time Life Pictures/Getty Images. 32-33: (eggs) PhotoDisc/Getty Images. 33: (t) (c)CORBIS (b) Ken Karp for MMH. 34: (t), (b) Hulton Archive/Getty Images. 34-35: (bkgd) Royalty Free/CORBIS. 35: (bkgd) Henryk T. Kaiser/Index Stock Imagery; (inset) ImageDJ/Alamy Images. 38: (b) John C.H. Grabill/(c)CORBIS. 39: (l) (c)Adam Woolfitt/CORBIS; (r) (c)Pat O'Hara/CORBIS. 40: (t) (c)Bettmann/CORBIS; (b) (c)Dave G. Houser/CORBIS. 41: (t) (c)Bettmann/CORBIS; (c) (c)Craig Aurness/CORBIS; (b) (c)Robert Holmes/CORBIS. 42: (t) American School/The Bridgeman Art Library; (b) The Granger Collection, New York. 43: (c) (c)Bettmann/CORBIS. 44: (l),(r) Ken Karp for MMH. 44-045: (r) Ken Karp for MMH. 45: (l) The Granger Collection, New York. 46-47: Ken Karp for MMH. 48: (l),(r) Ken Karp for MMH. 50-051: (b) (c)Minnesota Historical Society/CORBIS. 52: The Granger Collection, New York. 52-53: (t) The Granger Collection, New York. 53: The Granger Collection, New York. 54: (l) (c)Museum of the City of New York/CORBIS; (r) Philip Gendreau/(c)Bettmann/CORBIS. 55: (c)Bettmann/CORBIS. 56: The Granger Collection, New York. 58: (t) Courtesy of the Bancroft Library, University of California, Berkeley; (b) Ron Chapple/Thinkstock/Getty Images, Inc.. 58-59: Corbis. 59: (t) (c)The Newark Museum/Art Resource, NY; (b) Geoff Brightling/(c)Dorling Kindersley . 60: (cl) (c)Bettmann/CORBIS. 60-61: (b) Jeremy Woodhouse/Photodisc/Getty Images. 61: (l) (c)Bettmann/CORBIS; (r) John Wang/Photodisc/Getty Images. 62: (t) CheapShots/Alamy Images; (c) Davis Barber/Photo Edit Inc.; (b) (c)Ariel Skelley/Masterfile. 63: (t) (c)Kim Kulish/CORBIS. 64: (l) Susan Talbert. 65: (l),(r) Susan Talbert. 66: (inset) (c)Hulton-Deutsch Collection/CORBIS. 66-67: (bkgd) Tom Van Eynde/Panoramic Images. 67: (inset) Jean Dominique DALLET/Alamy Images. 68: (l) Courtesy of the Bancroft Library, University of California, Berkeley; (r) BananaStock/Punchstock. 69: The Granger Collection. 70: (c) (c) Bettmann/CORBIS. 70: (r) Courtesy of the Bancroft Library, University of California, Berkeley. 71: (all photos) Courtesy Lana Cheng. 72: MMH. 73: (bkgd) Carl Schneider/SHOTFILE.COM/Alamy Images. 74: Ken Karp for MMH. 75: (t) Mark Gibson/Index Stock Imagery; (b) Mark E. Gibson/MIRA: Media Image Resource Alliance. 80: (tl),(r) Chad Ehlers/Stone/Getty Images; (bl) (c)Douglas Slone/CORBIS. 81: (l) Bill Varie/CORBIS; (br) Robert Harding World Imagery/Getty Images, Inc.; (tr) Galen Rowell/CORBIS . 82: Lawrence Migdale/PIX. 84: (b) Ken Karp for MMH. 87: (t) Neal & Molly Jansen/SuperStock. 92: (inset) Mark E. Gibson/MIRA: Media Image Resource Alliance. 92-93: Robert Glusic/Photodisc/Getty. 93: (t) Mark Gibson/Index Stock Imagery. 94: (t) Mark E. Gibson/Unicorn Stock Photos. 94-95: Paul Barton/CORBIS. 95: (l) Lawrence Migdale/Photo Researchers, Inc.; (r) Siede Preis/Photodisc/Getty Images. 96: (b) Thinkstock/Punchstock. 98: (t) Ken Karp for MMH; (b) David Muench/CORBIS . 99: (l) Joe Robbins; (c) Darrell Gulin/CORBIS; (r) Robert Harding World Imagery/Getty Images, Inc.. 100: (l) Tom Mareschal/MIRA: Media Image Resource Alliance; (r) Prospectra/Spaceshots.com. 101: (l) Lee Foster/Bruce Coleman Inc.; (r) Joel Avila/Hawkeye Aerial Photography. 102: (l) Thomas Hallstein/Alamy Images. 102-103: (r) Barrie Rokeach/Aerial/Terrestrial Photography. 103: (l) Ken Karp for MMH; (tr) Joe Robbins/MIRA: Media Image Resource Alliance; (br) Tom Mareschal/MIRA: Media Image Resource Alliance. 104: (tl) Tom Mareschal/MIRA: Media Image Resource Alliance; (tr) David Muench/CORBIS; (bl) Darrell Gulin/CORBIS; (br) Robert Harding World Imagery/Getty Images, Inc.. 106-107: (bkgd) Carr Clifton / Minden Pictures. 108: (t) David A. Ponton/MIRA: Media Image Resource Alliance; (b) Royalty-Free/CORBIS. 109: (t) Bob Daemmrich/The Image Works, Inc.; (b) Michele/Tom Grimm. 110: David Young-Wolff/Photo Edit. 110-111: David Young-Wolff/Photo Edit. 112: U.S. Library of Congress. 112-113: John Elk III / Stock Boston. 113: (br) Bettmann/Corbis; (bl) JOHN MUIR PAPERS, HOLT-ATHERTON SPECIAL COLLECTIONS. UNIVERSITY OF THE PACIFIC LIBRARIES. COPYRIGHT 1984 MUIR-HANNA TRUST . 114-115: (bkgd) Geoff Bryant/Photo Researchers, Inc.. 114 (inset) Ken Karp for MMH. 115: (inset) Gregory G. Dimijian/Photo Researchers, Inc.. 116: Ken Karp for MMH. 118: Ken Karp for MMH. 128: (t) (c) Tom Bean/CORBIS; (b) Dave G. Houser/CORBIS . 128-129: (bkgd) Rob C. Williamson/Index Stock Imagery. 129: (tl) (c) W. Perry Conway/CORBIS; (br) John Elk III/Elk Photography. 130: (t) Hillel Burger/Peabody Museum of Archaeology and Ethnology/Harvard University (must be credited as above per Peabody Museum); (b) The Henry E. Huntington Library & Art Gallery. 132: (inset) (c)Bettmann/CORBIS. 132-133: (bkgd) Lomen Brothers/CORBIS. 133: photolibrary.com pty. ltd./Index Stock Imagery. 137: (t) (c)John Bigelow Taylor/Art Resource. 138: (t) Frank Krahmer/AGE Fotostock America; (c) Goodshoot/Picture Quest; (b) Spencer Grant/Photo Researchers, Inc.. 138-139: (b) Massimo Mastrorillo/CORBIS . 139: (t) Martin Harvey/Photo Researchers, Inc.; (c) R. van Nostrand/Photo Researchers, Inc.; (b) Martin Harvey/Photo Researchers, Inc.. 140: Photodisc/Getty Images, Inc.. 144: (t) MMH. 145: (c) N.Carter/North Wind Picture Archives. 146: Ken Karp. 147: (t) Brooks Kraft/CORBIS; (b) Reuters/CORBIS. 150: (r) (c) Royalty-Free/CORBIS; (tl) Jose Fuste Rage/AGE Fotostock America; (bl) Thomas M. Corcoran/AGE Fotostock America. 151: (l) Mark Wilson/Getty Images; (tr) Ron Sachs/CNP/CORBIS; (br) W. Bertsch/Robertstock/Retrofile. 155: (t) Jeff Greenberg/Omni-Photo Communications Inc.; (b) Royalty-Free/CORBIS. 156: Comstock Images/Getty Images, Inc.. 156-157: (c) Bettmann/CORBIS. 158:David Butow/CORBIS SABA/CORBIS. 158:Ted Soqui/Corbis. 160-161: (c) U.S. National Archives & Records Administration. 161: Burke/Triolo Productions/Brand X Pictures/Alamy. 162: (l), (r) The Granger Collection, New York. 163: (l) (c)Bettmann/CORBIS; (r) (c) SHAUN HEASLEY/Reuters/Corbis. 164: (b) (c) Bettmann/CORBIS. 164-165: (b) Tim Sloan/AFP/Getty Images. 166: J. Scott Applewhite/AP-Wide World Photos. 167: (l) Mark Wilson/Getty Images, Inc.; (c) Tim Sloan/AFP/Getty Images (r) J. Scott Applewhite/AP-Wide World Photos. 168: (l) (c)Gary Houlder/CORBIS. 169: Ken Karp for MMH. 170: (c)Royalty-Free/CORBIS. 170-171: José Fuste Raga/AGE Fotostock America. 171: Steve Allen/Brand X Pictures. 172: (l) Bettmann/CORBIS; (r) Photri/Microstock. 173: (l)Photri/Microstock; (r) Dirck Halstead/Time Life Pictures/Getty Images, Inc.. 174: (both photos) The Granger Collection, New York. 174-175: (c) Bettmann/CORBIS. 175: AFP/Getty Images, Inc.. 178-179: (t) Chuck Pefley/Alamy Images; (b) Elena Rooraid/Photoedit Inc.. 179: (t) (c) Robert Holmes/CORBIS; (b) Elena Rooraid/Photo Edit Inc.. 180: (b) (c) Kenneth James/Corbis. 181: (l) Marcio Sanchez/AP-Wide World Photos; (c) Paul Sakuma/AP-Wide World Photos; (r) Rich Pedroncelli/AP-Wide World Photos. 182: (b Royalty-Free/CORBIS. 192: (c) Barrett & MacKay Photography Inc.. 193: (l) Raffi Kirdi/Keystone Canada/Fraser Photos; (r) Tom Hanson/CP/AP-Wide World Photos. 194: Max Trujillo/Getty Images, Inc.. 194-195: (t) Jorge Uzon/AFP/Getty Images, Inc.; (b) Randy Faris/CORBIS. 196: (l) J. Neubauer/Robertstock/Retrofile; (r) Fritz Goro/Time Life Pictures/Getty Images, Inc.. 196-197: (bkgd) Mike Howell/Camerique Inc./Robertstock/Retrofile. 197: (inset) J. NeuBauer/Robertstock/Retrofile. 198: (bl) (c)Art Resource, NY. 199: Miguel Angel Munoz/PIXTAL/AGE Fotostock America. 201: (l) R. Kord/Robertstock/Retrofile; (r) David Rubinger/TIme Life Pictures/Getty Images, Inc.. 202: David Young-Wolff/Photo Edit Inc.. 203: Ben Welsh/AGE Fotostock America. 204-205: Creatas/Dynamic Graphics Group/Alamy Images. 205: Morales/AGE Fotostock America. 206: (l), (r) Ken Karp for MMH. 207: (c) qaphotos.com/ALAMY IMAGES. 208-209: Ken Karp for MMH. 209: (t) Reuters/CORBIS. 210: (c)Richard Cummins/CORBIS. 217: Becky Luigart-Stayner/Corbis. 218: Ken Karp for MMH. 219: (t) Kurt Wittman/Omni-Photo Communications Inc.; (b)(c) Don Mason/CORBIS. 226: (tl) David R. Frazier Photolibrary, Inc./Alamy Images; (bl) Mick Rock/Cephas Picture Library/Alamy; (r) David R. Frazier Photolibrary, Inc./Alamy Images. 227: (all photos) Pornchai Kittiwongsakul/AFP/Getty Images. 229: (l) Dennis MacDonald/A;amy Images; (c) David Hancock; (r) Don Gray/Photofusion Picture Library/Alamy Images. 230: Hub Willson/Robertstock. 231: (t) Mel Yates/Taxi/Getty Images. 232-(l) Ken Karp for MMH. 233: (both photos) Ken Karp for MMH. 234-235: (c)Ed Gifford/Masterfile. 237: (l) Morey Milbradt/Brand X Pictures/Alamy Images; (br) Stephen Schauer/Stone/Getty Images. 238: (c) Gianni Dagli Orti/CORBIS. 238-239: (t) Archivo Iconografico, S.A./Corbis. 239: (b) D. Hurst/Alamy Images. 240: (t) George Pickow/Three Lions/Hulton Archive/Getty Images; (bl) David Muench/Corbis; (br) Frank Kramer/Image State/Alamy. 241: (t) Peter Dean/Agripicture Images/Alamy Images; (b) (c) Tom Bean/CORBIS. 242: (t) Richard Hamilton Smith/Corbis; (b) Lionel Glyn/Bruce Coleman Inc.. 243: (l) Jacqui Hurst/Corbis; (r) Grant Faint/The Image Bank/Getty Images. 244: (l) Stone+/Getty Images; (r) Pavlovski Jacquez/Corbis Sygma/Corbis. 245: (l) Anthony Blake/Omni-Photo. 246: Stock Montage/Hulton Archive/Getty. 246-247: Hutton Archive/Getty Images. 247: (t) Steven Mark Needham/Foodpix; (b) Michael Barley/Corbis. 248: (l) Photodisc/Getty Images; (c) Barry Runk/Stan/Grant Heilman Photography, Inc.; (r) Dorling Kindersley/DK Images. 249: (t)(br) Royalty-Free from Disc/Corbis; (bl) James P. Blair/Photodisc Green/Getty Images. 250: (l) Michael Melford/The Image Bank/Getty Images; (r) Stephanie Maze/Corbis. 251: (t) Foodfolio/Alamy Images; (bl) (c) Walter Hodges/CORBIS; (br) Dennis MacDonald/Alamy Images. 252: (l) Harald Theissen/Imagebroker/Alamy Images; (r) Elizabeth Hathon/Corbis. 253: Burke/Triolo Productions/Brand X Pictures/Alamy Images. 256: (inset) Richard Hamilton Smith/Corbis. 256-257: (bkgd) Richard Price/Photographer's Choice/Getty. 257: (inset) Anthony Cooper: Ecoscene/Corbis. 258-259: (t) Nigel Cattlin/Holt Studios International LTD/Alamy Images; (b) (c) Bob Rowan; Progressive Image/CORBIS. 259: Lester Lefkowitz/Corbis. 260: (t) Paul Almasy/Corbis; (b) Kelly-Mooney Photography/Corbis. 261: (tl) John E. Kelly/Foodpix/Getty Images; (bl) Comstock Production/Comstock Images/Alamy Images; (r) Comstock Production Dept/Comstock Images/Alamy images. 264-265: G. Rossenbach/Masterfile Corporation. 265: (t) Chris Everard/Stone/Getty Images; (b) Photri/Microstock. 266: Royalty-free/Corbis. 266-267: Gerard Loucel/Stone/Getty Images. 268: Royalty-Free/Corbis. 268-269: (t) Farrell Grehan/Corbis; (b) Bruce Farnsworth/PlaceStockPhoto.com . 272: (l) Ken Karp for MMH; (c) J.A. Kraulis/Masterfile Corp.; (r) Photodisc/Corbis. 273: (t) Neil Beer/Photodisc Green/Getty Images; (b) Pictor International/Image State/Alamy Pictures/Alamy. 274: (r) Ken Karp for MMH. 275: (t) Eddie Stangler/Index Stock Photography. (b) Ken Karp for MMH. 276-277: Rick Sullivan/Bruce Coleman Inc.. 277: (t) Artville/Photodisc/Getty Images. 278: (t) Joseph Sohm/ChromoSohm Inc./Corbis; (bl) Richard Cummins/Corbis. 279: (c) Michael Pohuski/Foodpix. 278-279: (c) Kelly-Mooney Photography/CORBIS. 279: (t) Brett Shoaf / Intlcottages / Balboa Park Productions; (b)Arnold Gold/New Haven Register/The Image Works . 280: (b) Topham/The Image Works. 281: (t) Steve Cole/Getty Images; (b) Dave G. Houser/CORBIS. 282: Ian Murphy/Stone/Getty Images. 284: (l) H. Reinhard/Masterfile Corp.; (r) Danny Lehman/Corbis. 284-285: Danny Lehman/Corbis. 285: Juan Silva/Getty Images. 286: (t) Dinodia Photo/Getty Images; (b) Issouf Sanogo/AFP/Getty images. 286-287: (l) Pitchal Frederic/Corbis Sygma/Corbis. 287: Photodisc/Corbis. 288-289: (inset) Ken Karp for MMH; (background)(c) Royalty-Free/CORBIS. 290: Gary Braasch/Corbis. 290-291: Macduff Everton/The Image Bank/Getty Images. 291: Arvind Garg/Corbis. 292: Ingram Publishing/Alamy Images. 294: (l) Benelux Press/Stockfood America; (c) Lew Robertson/Foodpix; (r) Eising FoodPhotography / Stockfood America. 295: Ed Bock/Corbis. 297: (bl) (c)Steve Craft/Masterfile; (tl) Philip de Bay/(c)Historical Picture Archive/CORBIS; (cr) (c)Mitchell Gerber/CORBIS; (br) (c)Bettmann/CORBIS. (c) Bettmann/CORBIS; (tr) Penni Gladstone/San Francisco Chronicle/CORBIS. 298: (c)Jose Luis Pelaez, Inc./CORBIS. 299: (b) Milestones/Comstock Images; (t) Dave Schmidt/Masterfile. 302: (l)(r) (c) Reuters/CORBIS. (l) (c) Reuters/CORBIS. 303: (tr)(l) (c) Jonathan Blair/CORBIS; (br) (c) Louie Psihoyos/CORBIS. 304: C Squared Studios/Getty Images. 305: (bkgd) Alfred Eisenstaedt/Time Life Pictures/Getty Images; (inset) (c) Underwood & Underwood/CORBIS. 306: (bkgd)(inset) Bettmann/CORBIS. 307: (l) Kim Mould/Omni-Photo Communications, Inc.. 308: (r) Courtesy Birmingham Public Library Archives, Portrait Collection; (b) Science Museum/Science and Society Picture Library; (t) (c) CORBIS. 309: (t) The Granger Collection, New York; (b) Bettmann/CORBIS. 310: (tr) The Granger Collection; (tl) Burke/Triolo Productions/Brand X Pictures/Getty Images; (bl) Geostock/Getty Images; (br) Brian Hagiwara/Brand X Pictures/Getty Images, Inc.; (bc) Comstock Images/Getty Images, Inc.. 311: (tl) Burke/Triolo Productions/Brand X Pictures/Getty Images; (tr) Photolink/Getty Images; (bc) C Squared Studios/Getty Images; (tc) Ryan McVay/Photodisc/Getty Images, Inc.; (br) David Young-Wolff/PhotoEdit Inc.; (bl) (c) Rick Gayle Studio/CORBIS. 312-313: (b) Mike Dobel/Masterfile. 313: (b) Arlo K. Abrahamson/CHINFO, Navy Visual News Service/Photri Microstock; (t) Penni Gladstone/San Francisco Chronicle/CORBIS. 314: (t) Guy Cali/Alamy Images. 314-315: (b) Ed Bock/CORBIS. 315: Medical Professionals Disc/Comstock Images. 316: (b) PIXTAL/AGE Fotostock America. 316-317: (t) Bill Bachmann/The Image Works, Inc.. 317: (b) David Young-Wolff/Photo Edit. 318: (l) Courtesy of Denine Mayorga of Garden Grove, California; (r) Courtesy of Officer Richard Ward of the Lake County Sheriff's Department in Lake County, California. 319: Courtesy of Denine Mayorga of Garden Grove, California. 320: (l) Hulton Archive/Getty Images, Inc.. 321: (bl) Alfred Eisenstaedt/Time Life Pictures/Getty Images; (t) Courtesy of the Archives, California Institute of Technology; (br) Davies & Starr/The Image Bank/Getty Images. 322: (bl) Bettmann/CORBIS; (br) Photri Microstock. 322: (c)Bettmann/CORBIS. 323: (l) Paul Sakuma/AP-Wide World Photos; (r) Ed Kashi/CORBIS . 324: (tl) NASA/Photri Microstock; (inset) FOTOS Intl. /KEYSTONE Canada/ Fraser Photos; (bkgd) Taxi/Getty Images, Inc.; (t) Taxi/Getty Images, Inc.. 325: (b) M. Leon Bollee/Underwood & Underwood/CORBIS; (t) C.P. Cushing/Robertstock/Retrofile. 326: (c)ROB & SAS/CORBIS. 328: (all photos) Ken Karp for MMH. 328-329: (c) Hulton-Deutsch Collection/CORBIS. 329: Ken Karp for MMH. 330: (b) AP Photos/AP-Wide World Photos. 330-331: (c) William C. Shrout/Time Life Pictures/Getty Images. 331: Ken Karp for MMH. 332: (l) (c)Bettmann/CORBIS; (r) (c) Dr. David M. Phillips/Visuals Unlimited; (c) (c)The British Library/HIP/The Image Works. 333: (br) Ken Karp for MMH. 334: (l) David Sanger/Alamy Images; \(r) Ed Clark/Time Life Pictures/Getty Images, Inc.. 335: (br) Popperfoto/Alamy Images; (tr) The Granger Collection, New York; (tl) In the Garden, 1904 (pastel on paper), Cassatt, Mary Stevenson (1844-1926)/(c) The Detroit Institute of Arts, USA, Gift of Dr. Ernest Stillman; / www.bridgeman.co.uk ; (bl) (c)Erich Lessing / Art Resource, Inc. . 336: (t) F.S. & M.V. Fox, Chicago, Ill./Library of Congress; (c) Carqueville Litho Company/Library of Congress/Photri Microstock; (b) (c) Reuters/CORBIS. 337: (b) (c)Suki Coughlin Photography/Stylist: Paula McFarland; (t) Steven J. Polacco, 1999. 338: (r) Hulton Archive/Getty Images, Inc.; (l) Mario Tama/Getty Images, Inc.. 339: (b) (c) Rune Hellestad/CORBIS; (t) Hulton Archive/Getty Images. 340: (b) Tim Graham/CORBIS SYGMA/CORBIS; (t) Peter Kramer/Getty Images, Inc.. 341: (r) (c)FOX Photo/Entertainment Pictures/KEYSTONE Canada/Fraser Photos. 342: (r) Dr. Seuss Collection/Mandeville Special Collections Library/University of California, San Diegop; (l) Carlo Allegri/Getty Images. 343: Al Ravenna/New York World-Telegram and the Sun Newspaper Photograph Collection/Library of Congress. 344-345: (b) Alexander Gardner/ CORBIS. 345: (r) (c) Bettmann/CORBIS. 346: (t) The Granger Collection, New York; (b) AP - Wide World Photos. 347: (t) Corbis/Bettman; (b) Bettmann/CORBIS. 348: (l) Arthur Schatz/Time Life Pictures/Getty Images, Inc.; (bkgd) (c) Georgina Bowater/CORBIS. 349: (t) Gift of Ms. Tru S. Yasui, Japanese American National Museum (98.317.1) (must be credited as listed); (b) Russell Lee/CORBIS. 350: (r)(l) (c) Bettmann/CORBIS. 351: Apichart Weerawong/Reuters/Corbis. 352: (l) (c)Richard Cummins/CORBIS; (r) (c) Werner Forman/Art Resource, Inc.. 353: (b) (c)The Newark Museum/Art Resource, Inc.; (t) (c)Christie's Images/CORBIS. 354: (cl) ACQ/POPPERFOTO/Retrofile.com. 354-355: Donata Pizzi/The Image Bank/Getty Images. 355: Dinodia/AGE Fotostock America. 356: (b) (c)Flip Schulke/CORBIS. R1: Richard Price/Photographer's Choice/Getty Images. R4: (t) Lawrence Migdale for MMH. R5: David Young-Wolff/Alamy Images. R7: (c) Dennis Black/PictureQuest; (tl) Francis G. Mayer/CORBIS; (tr) CORBIS. R8: Arthur Schatz/Time Life Pictures/Getty Images. R9: Lori Adamski Peek/Stone/Getty Images. R10: Lawrence Migdale/Mira. R11: Michael Stevens/FogStock/Alamy Images. R12:(t) Mark Wilson/Getty Images. R13: Joe Chromo Sohn/PictureQuest. R24: (tc) J. Neubauer/Robertstock/Retrofile; (bc) Rune Hellestad/CORBIS; (b) Art Stein/Folio, Inc.. R25: (t) Jose Fuste Raga/AGE Fotostock America; (b) Alfred Eisenstaedt/Time Life Pictures/Getty Images. R26: (t to b) Jonathan Nourok/Photo Edit; Kim Kulish/CORBIS; Lee Foster/Bruce Coleman, Inc.; Charles & Josette Cenars/CORBIS. R27: (t to b) Brooks Kraft/CORBIS; (tc) U.S. National Archives & Records Administration; (bc) Alfredo Trombetta/Alinari Archives/CORBIS; (c) Ken Karp for MMH. R28: (t to b) Mike Dobel/Masterfile; Elena Rooraid/Photo Edit Inc.; Tom Bean/CORBIS; Davis Barber/Photo Edit, Inc.; Richard Price/Photographer's Choice/Getty Images; Robert Harding World Imagery/Getty Images, Inc.. R29: (t to b) AP Photos/AP-Wide World Photos; Joseph Sohm/CORBIS; Davies & Starr/The Image Bank/Getty Images; Pictor International/Image State/Alamy Pictures/Alamy; Pavlovski Jacquez/CORBIS Sygma/CORBIS. R30: (t to b) Bryan Allen/CORBIS; Harald Theissen/Imagebroker/Alamy; Kenneth James/CORBIS; Dave Mager for MMH. R31: (t to b) Penni Gladstone/San Francisco Chronicle/CORBIS; Creatas/Dynamic Graphics Group/Alamy Images; Topham/The Image Works, Inc.; CORBIS; Bettmann/CORBIS; Bob Daemmrich/Stock Boston; Ken Karp for MMH. R32: (t to b) M. Leon Bollee/Underwood & Underwood/CORBIS; Royalty-Free/CORBIS; Prospectra/Spaceshots.com; US District Court/AP Wide World Photos; John Neubauer/PhotoEdit Inc.; Barrie Rokeach/Aerial/Terrestrial Photography. R33: (c) Ken Karp for MMH; (b) Richard Cummins/CORBIS. R34: (t to b) David Muench/CORBIS; Richard Quataert/Folio Inc.; Hub Willson/Robertstock/Retrofile; Tom Mareschal/MIRA: Media Image Resource Alliance; CORBIS; Nigel Cattlin/Holt Studios International LTD/Alamy Images. R35: (t to b) Joel Avila/Hawkeye Aerial Photogrpahy; Darrell Gulin/CORBIS; Shaun Heasley Reuters/CORBIS; Ken Karp for MMH; Ken Karp for MMH. R36: (t) David Young-Wolff/Photo Edit; (bc) Thomas Hallstein/Alamy Images; (b) Robert Glusic/Photodisc/Getty Images, . R37: (t to b) Ken Karp for MMH; Ken Karp for MMH; Hulton Archive/Getty Images; Ed Bock/CORBIS; Kurt Wittman/Omni-Photo Communications Inc.. R38: (t) Alexander Gardner/CORBIS; (tc) Ken Karp for MMH; (c) Farrell Grehan/CORBIS; (bc) Mark Gibson/Index Stock Imagery; (b) Royalty-Free/CORBIS. R39: (tc) Paul Sakuma/AP-Wide World Photos; (bc) Ian Murphy/Stone/Getty Images. R40: (t to b) Comstock Production Department/Comstock Images/Alamy Images; Mark E. Gibson/MIRA: Media Image Resource Alliance; Joe Robbins/MIRA: Media Image Resource Alliance; PIXTAL/AGE Fotostock America; Mel Yates/Taxi/Getty Images. R41: (t) Library of Congress; (b) Steve Allen/Brand X Pictures.

★ ACKNOWLEDGMENTS ★

Grateful acknowledgment is given to the following authors and publishers. Every effort has been made to trace the ownership of all copyrighted material and to secure the necessary permissions to reprint these selections. In the case of some selections for which acknowledgment is not given, extensive research has failed to locate the copyright holders.

Children of Long Ago, from "Children of Long Ago." Text by Lessie Jones Little. Illustrations by Jan Spivey Gilchrist. Text Copyright © 1988 Lessie Jones Little. Illustrations Copyright © 1988 Jan Spivey Gilchrist. Published by Philomel Books, A Division of the Putnam & Grossett Group. All Rights Reserved. Used by Permission.

Josefina Fierro de Bright, from 1983 Interview by Mario T. Garcia, Professor of History and Chicano Studies, University of California, Santa Barbara. Used by Permission.

Cover permission for **Abuela**, Text by Arthur Dorro. Illustrations by Elisa Kleven. Text Copyright © 1991 by Arthur Dorros. Illustrations Copyright © 1991 by Elisa Kleven. Published by the Penguin Group. All Rights Reserved.

Cover permission for **Sarah Morton's Day: A Day in the Life of a Pilgrim Girl**, Text by Kate Waters. Illustrations by Russell Kendall. Text Copyright © 1989 by Kate Waters. Illustrations Copyright © 1989 by Russell Kendall. Published by Scholastic, Inc. All Rights Reserved. Used by permission.

Cover permission for **Grandfather's Journey**, Text and Illustrations by Allen Say. Copyright © 1993 by Allen Say. Published by Houghton Mifflin Company. All Rights Reserved.

John Muir, from Wilderness Society website: www.wilderness.org/Library/Documents/Beauty_Quotes.cfm Used by Permission.

Cover permission for **Our Earth**, by Judith Caseley. Copyright © 2002 by Judith Caseley. Published by Greenwillow Books, An Imprint of HarperCollins Publishers. All Rights Reserved.

Cover permission for **On the Town**, Written and Illustrated by Anne Rockwell. Copyright © 1998 by Anne Rockwell. Published by Harcourt, Inc. All Rights Reserved.

Cover permission for **Garbage and Recycling**, by Rosie Harlow & Sally Morgan. Copyright © 2001 by Kingfisher Publications, A Houghton Mifflin Company imprint. All Rights Reserved.

Golda Meir, from "As Good As Golda" compiled and edited by Israel and Mary Shenker. Copyright © 1970 by Israel and Mary Shenker. Published by McCall Publishing Company. All Rights Reserved. Used by Permission.

Cover permission for **Jamaica Louise James**, Text by Amy Hest. Illustrations by Sheila White Samton. Text Copyright © 1996 by Amy Hest. Illustrations Copyright © 1996 by Sheila White Samton. Published by Candlewick Press. All Rights Reserved.

Cover permission for **Duck for President**, Text by Doreen Cronin. Illustrations by Betsy Lewin. Text Copyright © 2004 by Doreen Cronin. Illustrations Copyright © 2004 by Betsy Lewin. Published by Simon & Schuster Books For Young Readers. All Rights Reserved.

Cover permission for **Woodrow the White House Mouse**, Text and Illustrations by Peter Barnes and Cheryl Shaw Barnes. Copyright © 1998 by Peter Barnes and Cheryl Shaw Barnes. Published by VSP Books. All Rights Reserved.

Farmworkers, from "Gathering the Sun: An Alphabet in Spanish and English." Text by Alma Flor Ada, English translation by Rosa Zubizarreta. Illustrations by Simon Silva. Copyright © 1997 Alma Flor Ada. Published by Lothrop, Lee & Shepard Books, A Division of William Morrow & Company, Inc. All Rights Reserved. Used by Permission.

George Washington Carver, from "George Washington Carver in His Own Words" edited by Gary R. Kremer. Copyright © 1991 by the University of Missouri Press. Used by Permission.

Cover permission for **Click Clack Moo**, Text by Doreen Cronin. Illustrations by Betsy Lewin. Text Copyright © 2000 by Doreen Cronin. Illustrations Copyright © 2000 by Betsy Lewin. Published by Simon & Schuster Books For Young Readers. All Rights Reserved.

Cover permission for **How to Make an Apple Pie and See the World**, Text by Marjorie Priceman. Copyright © 1994 by Marjorie Priceman. Dragonfly Books™ Published by Alfred A. Knopf, Inc. All Rights Reserved.

Cover permission for **Bread, Bread, Bread**, Text by Ann Morris. Photographs by Ken Heyman. Text Copyright © 1989 by Ann Morris. Photographs Copyright © 1989 by Ken Heyman. Published by HarperCollins Publishers. All Rights Reserved.

Hold Fast to Your Dreams, from "This Place I Know: Poems of Comfort." Text by Louise Driscoll, Selected by Georgia Heard. This collection Copyright © 2002 by Georgia Heard. Published by Candlewick Press. All Rights Reserved. Used by Permission.

Abraham Lincoln, from "Abraham Lincoln: Speeches and Writings, 1859 – 1865." Copyright © 1989 by The Claremont Institute. Used by Permission.

Cover permission for **I Am Rosa Parks**, Text by Rosa Parks with Jim Haskin. Illustrations by Wil Clay. Text Copyright © 1997 by Rosa Parks. Illustrations Copyright © 1997 by Wil Clay. Published by Puffin Books, the Penguin Group. All Rights Reserved.

Cover permission for **Firefighters**, Text by Jill C. Wheeler. Copyright © 2003 by Abdo Consulting Group, Inc. Published by ABDO Publishing Company. All Rights Reserved.

Cover permission for **Diego**, Text by Jonah Winter. Illustrations by Jeanette Winter. Text Copyright © 1991 by Jonah Winter. Illustrations Copyright © 1991 Jeanette Winter. Published by Alfred A. Knopf, Inc. All Rights Reserved.

Historical and Social Sciences Analysis Skills

Chronological and Spatial Thinking

1. Students place key events and people of the historical era they are studying in a chronological sequence and within a spatial context; they interpret time lines.

2. Students correctly apply terms related to time, including *past, present, future, decade, century,* and *generation.*

3. Students explain how the present is connected to the past, identifying both similarities and differences between the two, and how some things change over time and some things stay the same.

4. Students use map and globe skills to determine the absolute locations of places and interpret information available through a map's or globe's legend, scale, and symbolic representations.

5. Students judge the significance of the relative location of a place (e.g., proximity to a harbor, on trade routes) and analyze how relative advantages or disadvantages can change over time.

Research, Evidence, and Point of View

1. Students differentiate between primary and secondary sources.

2. Students pose relevant questions about events they encounter in historical documents, eyewitness accounts, oral histories, letters, diaries, artifacts, photographs, maps, artworks, and architecture.

3. Students distinguish fact from fiction by comparing documentary sources on historical figures and events with fictionalized characters and events.

Historical Interpretation

1. Students summarize the key events of the era they are studying and explain the historical contexts of those events.

2. Students identify the human and physical characteristics of the places they are studying and explain how those features form the unique character of those places.

3. Students identify and interpret the multiple causes and effects of historical events.

4. Students conduct cost-benefit analyses of historical and current events.

History–Social Science Content Standards
Grade 2 People Who Make a Difference

2.1 Students differentiate between things that happened long ago and things that happened yesterday.

1. Trace the history of a family through the use of primary and secondary sources, including artifacts, photographs, interviews, and documents.

2. Compare and contrast their daily lives with those of their parents, grandparents, and/or guardians.

3. Place important events in their lives in the order in which they occurred (e.g., on a time line or storyboard).

2.2 Students demonstrate map skills by describing the absolute and relative locations of people, places, and environments.

1. Locate on a simple letter-number grid system the specific locations and geographic features in their neighborhood or community (e.g., map of the classroom, the school).

2. Label from memory a simple map of the North American continent, including the countries, oceans, Great Lakes, major rivers, and mountain ranges. Identify the essential map elements: title, legend, directional indicator, scale, and date.

3. Locate on a map where their ancestors live(d), telling when the family moved to the local community and how and why they made the trip.

4. Compare and contrast basic land use in urban, suburban, and rural environments in California.

2.3 Students explain governmental institutions and practices in the United States and other countries.

1. Explain how the United States and other countries make laws, carry out laws, determine whether laws have been violated, and punish wrongdoers.

2. Describe the ways in which groups and nations interact with one another to try to resolve problems in such areas as trade, cultural contacts, treaties, diplomacy, and military force.

2.4 Students understand basic economic concepts and their individual roles in the economy and demonstrate basic economic reasoning skills.

1. Describe food production and consumption long ago and today, including the roles of farmers, processors, distributors, weather, and land and water resources.

2. Understand the role and interdependence of buyers (consumers) and sellers (producers) of goods and services.

3. Understand how limits on resources affect production and consumption (what to produce and what to consume).

2.5 Students understand the importance of individual action and character and explain how heroes from long ago and the recent past have made a difference in others' lives (e.g., from biographies of Abraham Lincoln, Louis Pasteur, Sitting Bull, George Washington Carver, Marie Curie, Albert Einstein, Golda Meir, Jackie Robinson, Sally Ride).